DAD THE FAMILY
COUNSELOR

◆

DAVE SIMMONS

VICTOR BOOKS ®

A DIVISION OF SCRIPTURE PRESS PUBLICATIONS INC.
USA CANADA ENGLAND

SERIES

Dad, the Family Shepherd
P.O. Box 21445
Little Rock, AR 72221
(501) 221-1102

All Scripture references are from the *New American Standard Bible,* © the Lockman Foundation 1960, 1962, 1963, 1968, 1971, 1972, 1973, 1975, 1977. Used by permission.

Library of Congress Cataloging-in-Publication Data

Simmons, Dave.
    Dad the family counselor / David A. Simmons.
      p. cm. —(Dad the family shepherd)
    ISBN 0-89693-947-2
    1. Fathers—Religious life. 2. Fatherhood (Christian theology)
3. Family—Religious life. I. Title. II. Series: Simmons, Dave. Dad the family
shepherd.
BV4843.S57   1991   91-25023
248.8'421—dc20   CIP

DAD THE FAMILY
COUNSELOR

Contents

DAD THE FAMILY SHEPHERD SERIES

WISDOM

PHILOSOPHY

WHAT YOU MUST KNOW — **WHAT YOU MUST BE**

SIGNIFICANCE				SCOPE			
1	2	3	4	5	6	7	8

FUNCTIONS

SURVEY OF FUNCTIONS

VOLUME 1 — DAD the FAMILY COACH

PRACTICAL

TECHNIQUES

WHAT YOU MUST DO — **COACHING TIPS**

LOVE	BOND			LEAD			
1	2	3	4	5	6	7	8

VOLUME 2 — DAD the FAMILY COUNSELOR

EQUIP

TEACH		TRAIN		TRACK		TEND	
1	2	3	4	5	6	7	8

VOLUME 3 — DAD the FAMILY MENTOR

Dedication

To my wife:
Sandy Willey Simmons

Wife • Friend • Lover • Counselor • Mother of our children

She tries harder than anyone I have ever known

Coaching Tips:
How to get the most from this book

Coaching Tip One: START AN E-TEAM.
Real Men Need Real Men

Dad, the Family Shepherd
E-TEAM

Iron sharpens iron, so one man sharpens another.
—Proverbs 27:17

For best results, this course on fatherhood should be:

1. Ingested internally at the rate of one chapter per week.
2. Digested in the company of a few trusted men, an E-Team.
3. Invested in the lives of your family slowly but surely.

This calls for an E-Team (Encouragement Team), a small group of five–seven men who meet weekly to study family-life principles and to motivate each other to apply what they learn. An E-Team functions as a vehicle to get you from the valley of intention to the plateau of success. An E-Team converts ambition to action. It transfers desire for better fatherhood to changed behavior patterns in the home.

An E-Team is the only way I know to guarantee steady progress. There are no shortcuts. Progress requires men committed to help each other work hard at fatherhood over a long period of time.

Take the initiative and recruit an E-Team to go through this course with you.

An E-Team gives a man:

> Encouragement
> Understanding
> Inspiration
> Solutions
> Challenge
> Accountability

E-TEAM INSTRUCTIONS

In order to establish an E-Team and successfully lead it through this course, follow these steps.

1. ACQUIRE THE E-TEAM CAPTAIN'S MANUAL IN VOLUME I: *DAD THE FAMILY COACH* OR SEND TO DAD THE FAMILY SHEPHERD FOR IT.

2. RECRUIT YOUR TEAM.

Challenge four to six other men to meet together with you for eight weeks to complete the course. Mention that each meeting has a reading assignment that must be completed beforehand and there will be a brief, practical, useful application project following each session. Make sure each man gets a copy of the book in time to prepare for the first meeting.

3. MAKE ASSIGNMENTS.

Instruct each man to read "The Scouting Report" and Chapter 1: "Dad the Family Encourager" before the first meeting. Remind them to bring the book, notepaper, and pencil to the meeting.

4. FOLLOW THE E-TEAM GUIDE AT THE END OF EACH SESSION.

At the meeting, just follow the E-Team Guide at the end of each session.

Coaching Tip Two: STUDY THE CONTEXT.

Overview of the Dad the Family Shepherd Series

> Volume One: *Dad the Family Coach*
> Volume Two: *Dad the Family Counselor*
> Volume Three: *Dad the Family Mentor*

Foreword

Peter, the CEO of a national brokerage firm, had a sparkling career that was more successful than he had ever dreamed. He had risen to the top because he had devoted his life to being "the best" executive he could be.

In spite of his accomplishments at work, he felt like a failure at home. His first two wives left him, his third was on her way out, and his son rebelled and plunged himself into the drug counterculture. The more Peter's business came together, the more his family fell apart.

The chief complaint from Peter's family centered on his inability to develop intimate relationships. His family used these terms to describe him: coldhearted, uncaring, insensitive, bossy, dictator, dominating, critical, etc.

Peter knew he had something inside him that would not allow him to build healthy, loving relationships, but he did not know what it was. He never realized that his inability to touch the hearts of those he loved could be related to how his father crushed his heart as a youngster. His neglectful father left a deep feeling of abandonment and isolation that formed the core of his self-image for today and profoundly affected his relationships.

In another case, Julia, an unusually attractive cheerleader in college who became an airline stewardess, met her husband on an international flight. After a quick and passionate romance they were married. A few years rolled by and they had a child. She began to resent the sexual aspect of her marriage and developed an attitude that sex was a punishment she needed to endure because of her fast-track lifestyle in college. At the same time, she began to worry about her beauty. She began to suspect that her good looks were beginning to fade.

She developed an obsession with food and believed that she needed to lose weight to regain her former beauty and that sense of euphoria that came when men paid attention to her. She started losing weight and became anorexic. Her problems multiplied.

Julia's father set the tone for her lifetime relationship with men. He demanded perfection from her in every aspect of life. She could never please him. He never passed out compliments: the best she could ever expect in terms of encouragement was the absence of condemnation. He also failed to provide the emotional nourishment a young girl needs to feel good about her femininity. She was starved for father-love and turned to the superficial sensual relationships with her many boyfriends to fill the longing in her heart.

These case studies are just two of thousands that we encounter at RAPHA, our nationwide system of Christian hospital treatment centers. In the many years we have practiced Christian counseling, we have encountered every problem that mankind can develop. In spite of the diversity of the problems, almost all of them share one thing in common—they developed these disorders (or at least the propensity for them) while growing up in a dysfunctional family.

These disorders are symptoms: the problem that causes these symptoms arises from the terrible shame and pain these people suffered as children. They did not know how to process the pain they experienced in a dysfunctional family, and they groped for systems that would grant any relief at all.

As I wrote in *The Search for Significance:*

Human beings develop elaborate defense mechanisms to block pain and gain significance. We suppress emotions; we are compulsive perfectionists; we drive ourselves to succeed, or withdraw and become passive; we attack people who hurt us; we punish ourselves when we fail; we try to say clever things to be accepted; we help people so that we will be appreciated; and we say and do countless other things.

Some of us have deep emotional and spiritual scars resulting from the neglect, abuse, and manipulation that often accompany living in a dysfunctional family (alcoholism, drug abuse, divorce, absent father or mother, excessive anger, verbal and/or physical abuse, etc.).

Many of us must struggle for the rest of our lives trying to convert our shame-based identity for a healthy honor-based identity. In the process, many of us from dysfunctional families pass the pain and dysfunction onto the next generation because we have not learned how to overcome our own damage. We do not know how to break the cycle—to stop the negative spiral down through the generations and replace it with a soaring positive system. It can be done. It has been done.

The Dad the Family Shepherd Series by Dave Simmons tells how it can be done in a practical way. It presents a trustworthy system of parenting principles presented in the context of fatherhood. Dave

Simmons has written a course that covers the basics of wellness fathering. The expressed goal of this series is to equip men to perform their fathering functions with excellence so that the children will grow up with healthy spiritual and emotional stability.

By approaching the family through the avenue of "wellness fathering," this series will help men establish healthy homes and avoid the dysfunctions that cause children to develop the personality disorders which proliferate in our country.

This book, *Dad the Family Counselor*, addresses three key elements in promoting emotional health and positive self-esteem in children:

1. How to LOVE your child which establishes significance in the child.
2. How to BOND your child which establishes belongingness in the child.
3. How to LEAD your child which helps a child establish identity.

A child growing up under a nurturing father who has perfected the skills of providing the above will stand a much better chance of adjusting to the stress and trials they will face in the twenty-first century. In this time of absent fathers, children need "father power" more than ever.

In a time of family turbulence and social tumult our families are in danger of being flooded and washed away by currents of our culture. Confusion reigns in our land when it comes to family norms, gender roles, and child-raising systems. Dave Simmons has given fathers a fresh, dynamic message on fatherhood. This book is an anchor that will help you stabilize your family. Master the principles in this volume with other good men in your church and let your children reap the benefits through the years.

Robert S. McGee
President and Founder of
RAPHA

The Scouting Report

"In the 1960s and 1970s the entire structure of the family has begun to shift. The nuclear family is crumbling—to be replaced, I think, by the free floating couple, a marital dyad subject to dramatic fissions and fusions, and without the orbiting satellites of pubertal children, close friends or neighbors . . . just the relatives, hovering in the background, friendly smiles on their faces."
—Ed Shorter

WILD, WILD FATHERHOOD

When I was five years old, my family lived in on-post housing at Ft. Knox, Kentucky. Every afternoon, at quitting time, I stationed myself on the front porch as the lookout for Dad. He came home at irregular times because he passed the NCO club on his walk home. When he did approach, he had to walk down a long slope, cross a footbridge, and march up a long flight of steps to get to our house. My job consisted of observing his passage over the uneven terrain before our house to determine if he was drunk.

If it looked bad, I flew through the house like a midget air raid system to alert everyone. I waited in the kitchen at the head of the basement stairs. Everyone waited in fearful suspense to see what would happen. You never knew. Dad was an unpredictable drunk. Sometimes, he bubbled into the living room with smiles and cheers for everyone. Most of the time, the door opened and slammed back against the wall and Dad walked in glaring at us in screaming silence.

The family scrambled. I liked to bail out down the stairs and hide in the basement. Poor Mom. She always held her ground and faced him head-on to give us a chance to hide out. I can remember trembling in the shadowy dank basement for hours waiting for the storm to blow over.

Sometimes, I didn't escape. There has never been anything in my life that upset me more than the cold-clutching clammy fear I felt

14

grip me when Dad turned his fever on me.

Afterward, Dad could be the nicest man in the world. You could not imagine the regret, sorrow, and shame he felt. He would hold us, sometimes crying, and apologize over and over. I can vividly remember his giant lumberjack hands pressing me against his brass buttons and campaign ribbons and smelling his beer dampened wool uniform. I squeezed my little chest to let escape great gobs of sorrowful whimpers. It confused me so. I didn't understand.

Naturally, I developed ambivalent feelings toward Dad. I harbored a love/hate, crave/reject, fear/comfort kind of attitude toward him. These feelings toward the dominant male authority figure in my life became locked into me and, later in life, every time I encountered an authority figure, these feelings resurfaced. I grabbed the network of feelings toward Dad, lifted them up, and settled them down on any authority in front of me. I have never done well with coaches, professors, or bosses.

Bad dads make bad kids. A dysfunctional dad causes a dysfunctional family which produces dysfunctional children. Negative father power rolls on and transfers the sins of a father to the children, even the second, third, and fourth generations. A bad dad can poison his seed.

I grew up thinking that we had the only unhappy family. I thought we had some rare family affliction that all other families were vaccinated against. They all seemed so healthy and happy. It never occurred to me the greater the dysfunction, the greater the family tries to hide it. Many other families hid their anguish behind carefully constructed masks just like we did.

When I started my own family, I struggled with my role as a father. I did not have the strength in the inner man, the character and integrity good fatherhood requires, nor did I possess the skills of father-craft and father-lore that have been passed down through the generations. I needed help but there was not much available. I had to learn mostly from trial and error in the crucial early years and, later on, I was able to get professional help.

I believe most men are like me and can benefit from a common-sense approach that lends itself to easy application and measurable positive results. The principles and techniques in this book changed my life. They worked for me. And I think we are a lot alike in many ways so I predict that you will make significant advances in your family shepherding skills if you study this book; especially if you study it with a small team of men.

As a result of my experience in a dysfunctional family of origin, my twenty years of work at King's Arrow Ranch (a youth camp), my years of research and study on the family in graduate school, my years with the Family Ministry of Campus Crusade for Christ, and my term as father to Helen and Brandon, I have seen the good side and bad side of fatherhood. I have played the victim, the failure, the champion, the observer, the counselor, and the spokesman for fatherhood.

My experience with fatherhood from these many different angles compels me to make fatherhood the great cause of my life. I am unashamedly a fatherhood activist. A fatherist. The driving force in my life at this time is to see fatherhood, the oldest profession, be restored to the lofty status God intends it to be and to be practiced with excellence.

WELLNESS FATHERHOOD

As you consider your role as a father, it helps to know the different states of fatherhood and which one best matches your situation. The three states of entry into the fatherhood movement:

1. Wellness Fatherhood Training—Training for pre-fathers and new fathers designed to equip them with a philosophy and skills that will help them perform well from the beginning.
2. Enhancement Fatherhood Training—Training to sustain fathers as family situations continually change and to help fathers make adjustments and corrections that will improve fathering.
3. Remedial Fatherhood Training—Training for fathers who find themselves on the wrong track, faced with devastating problems, or in a crisis and in need of serious, sometimes professional, assistance.

Dad the Family Shepherd overwhelmingly focuses on Wellness Fatherhood Training with an emphasis on Enhancement Training. The three volumes in the Dad the Family Shepherd Series concentrate on Wellness Fatherhood Training. This is like preventative care for fathers. I write on family construction—how to build it right the first time.

A primary book on fathering would naturally deal with the ideal family and the fathering techniques that build a healthy, stable family. It could not possibly address all of the unique family pathologies to which dysfunctional families are prone. It deals with how to take the essential steps to keep your family well and avoid serious problems on down the line.

Remedial, correctional, and rehabilitation fatherhood are more advanced topics but they too require the mastering of Wellness Fathering as part of the solution. We also help with assessment. But, for serious childhood, fatherhood, and family problems that require more sophisticated therapy and reclamation techniques, I refer you to your pastor, and specially equipped counseling agencies like RAPHA, Minirth/Meier, and others.

FORECASTED FATHERHOOD

Dan Dantzler, President of Dad the Family Shepherd board of directors, drove his immaculate little pickup toward the golf course and told me, "Dave, I sure would like to play golf with you more often and get my golf game up to par but I just can't. I got to pull my fatherhood tour-of-duty. I figure I got about eighteen more months of high-intensive fathering to do before I can loosen up."

"What?" I replied.

"Yeah. Until I get my kids past two, I have to do double-time fatherhood. They need me a lot right now."

Ole Dan put his golf game on hold until he got through this demanding period of fatherhood. I, on the other hand, am blissfully floating in the golden age of fatherhood: both kids out of the house and I am free, free, free. What a relief! Now, I can just sit around and pontificate about fathering—I don't have to do it! Just kidding. I still have major fathering to do and will for some time. In fact, a father can't ever stop worrying about his kids!

This brings up an important point: There are definite stages in the fathering life cycle. Research by Ken Canfield (1990), Director of the National Center for Fathering, shows five stages of fatherhood based on men's feelings of fathering satisfaction. These stages coincide with the age of the oldest child.

1. Age of Idealism. (Child age—1–6)
This is the age of unrealistic fatherhood. Fathers are lulled into a low maintenance mode because they think the children's demands are not serious. Dad needs to get his career on track and his marriage settled and thinks the kids won't need strong fathering

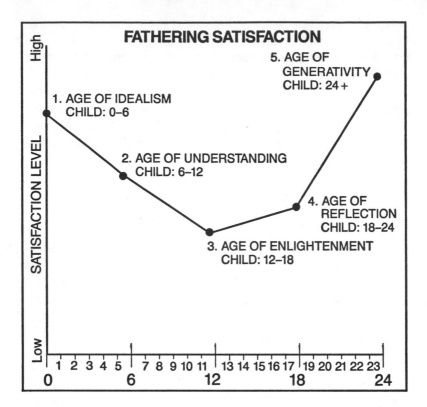

FATHERING SATISFACTION

1. AGE OF IDEALISM
CHILD: 0–6

2. AGE OF UNDERSTANDING
CHILD: 6–12

3. AGE OF ENLIGHTENMENT
CHILD: 12–18

4. AGE OF REFLECTION
CHILD: 18–24

5. AGE OF GENERATIVITY
CHILD: 24+

until the kids get involved with bigger problems. Dads feel high fathering satisfaction because they are coasting and don't get any negative feedback for it. Yet.

2. Age of Understanding. (Child age—6–12)
Reality sobers up fathers. The demands become greater and the problems greater. But the children are at the fun "kid stage." The regular system of fathering habits are set as men get into the role.

3. Age of Enlightenment. (Child age—12–18)
The pits. Teens run wild as hormones go berserk! Teens get old and strong enough to express themselves, regardless. Dads can't overpower them anymore and must negotiate. Teen problems get painful and expensive and absorb more of your energy. This coincides with the highest point in marital dissatisfaction. This is the lowest ebb in a man's life and can lead easily to a crisis if not anticipated and prepared for.

4. Age of Reflection. (Child age — 18–24)
I'm out of the pits. Relief. I don't have to struggle with active fathering but I do suffer from painful memories and regrets. Usually, the children begin to come around and start owning the values we have been promoting. However, there are so many of this age-group who are literally staying in the home these days, that a label has been coined for them — tweenagers. Of course, this complicates the fathering lifestyle.

5. Age of Generativity. (Child age — 24+)
When a man's children are up and out, he feels a need to reach out and make a mark on society. He no longer struggles with active fathering and puts himself out as a consultant and adviser. He turns to the delightful role of secondary fathering — grandfathering. All of the pleasure without the pain.

OPTIMISTIC FATHERHOOD

Whichever state and age of fatherhood you find yourself in, take heart! A fatherhood awakening looms on the horizon. Men are stirring themselves and reevaluating their priorities and getting serious about fatherhood.

I am convinced that we will see a major Old Testament prophecy fulfilled in our lifetimes. Malachi, in the last sentence of the Old Testament, predicted that, at a certain time, there would be a universal rejuvenation of fatherhood. "And he will restore the hearts of the fathers to their children, and the hearts of the children to their fathers, lest I come and smite the land with a curse" (4:6).

Such an event has never happened and I believe that it is long overdue and will happen soon. I believe that we will see a major, grass roots movement of men back to the strategic profession of fatherhood. I believe it will start in the churches, spread throughout our culture, and leap to other countries. This is the confidence that we, at Dad the Family Shepherd, and many other fatherhood ministries, have: We are part of a vast operation that will restore the fellowship between fathers and their children.

The purpose of the Dad the Family Shepherd Series is to help fathers see the seriousness of fatherhood, understand the details of their assignment, and master the techniques of fathering with excellence. If you take fatherhood seriously and study this book with a few other good men, you will capture the essence of fatherhood and master the techniques of basic family shepherding.

The Fatherhood Function: To Love

Chapter One
Dad the Family
Encourager

*"The basic cause of all mental and emotional
illness is the inability to form deep human
relationships of love. There is a universal
agreement that the amount of affection received in
infancy determines, more than any other
influence, the whole course and quality of
human life."*

—John Powell

I LOVE YOU
10,000 GUINEA PIGS WORTH!

My daughter, Helen, taught me about the love language of children. I was sleeping soundly in my bed early one morning when abruptly I had an unconscious premonition of an alien presence in my room. I felt watched. I snapped open my eyes and found two giant soft brown eyeballs staring at me from about six inches away. It was Helen. My little five-year-old daughter had crept in bed to be with her daddy and had lain there just staring at me and thinking about me.

Before I could respond, she blurted, "Daddy, I love you 10,000 guinea pigs worth!"

"Ten thousand guinea pigs?" To my sleepy mind, drowning in an undulating sea of tricolor guinea pigs did not elicit thoughts of tender affection. "What's wrong with this kid? She loves me like a pig?"

It gradually dawned on me, as she lay there in the wee hours of the morning, that she had just confessed love to me in terms that expressed the ultimate degree of love to her. She had recently acquired two baby guinea pigs, whom she loved with all her little

23

feminine heart. It took me a little while to translate it, but when I did, it nearly overwhelmed me to think that her affection for me equaled ten thousand times her affection for one of her little piggies.

She chose guinea pigs as her medium of exchange to express her love. As she lay there watching her old man sleeping (tells you how exciting things were around our house!), she pondered the depths of her love for her dad. She had these tender feelings for him that made her feel good inside and want to say and do nice things for him.

As she savored these delicious emotions, she measured them and figured out how to convey them to her dad. She made the association with the feelings she had for her dad with those she had for the little pigs. She measured her love, calculated its value in guinea pigs, and made her transaction. Helen spoke to me in her own private love language.

It is not enough just to love your family; they need to find out about it. You need to convert your love into a language they can interpret. Every child has a unique specific set of expressions and actions that mean love to them. You need to find out each child's love language and learn to converse in it fluently.

Every child has a unique way to perceive love, and they all share a common need for it. Children dry up and die without it. Some experiments were done in Russia in the nineteenth century to see what language a child would speak if no one ever spoke to that child. Scores of orphaned babies were put into a love sterile environment with neither communication nor love. Only their physical needs were met. Not one of them lived longer than a year; most of them died within a few months. Love is a life and death issue.

THE HUNGER OF LOVE

I listed love as the first major function because it constitutes the foundation to all the other functions of a family shepherd. Love must permeate the rest of your responsibilities. Love determines the style and modus operandi of the other functions—Bond, Lead, and Equip.

Love also represents the most significant need of your wife. After over twenty years of family ministry, Sandy and I have discovered that the overwhelming complaint of wives is the lack of love from their husbands. Something's wrong. Either men are not loving their wives or they do but have no clue as to how to communicate it. Whichever it is, love is not registering with the women.

Twenty years at King's Arrow Ranch working with over 8,000 children from all classes has convinced Sandy and me that the number one factor in the lives of children is parental love. We soon learned the skill of determining what kind of parents a child has within a few minutes, sometimes by simply observing how the kids get out of a car and approach the Ranch House during registration. Love-starved children wear their needs on their faces. Anyone, with a little experience, can soon learn to read about parents in a child's face.

During my first year as director of King's Arrow Ranch, I was stunned to discover how love-deprived children literally cling to a loving male dominant authority figure. A small nine-year-old boy living in the Dodge City bunkhouse shied away from me constantly, especially at mealtime in the Ranch House. It took a week to get him to let me approach him. I finally managed to pick him up and hold him. I just kept looking him in the eye and smiling. Before the camping session was over, I thought I had a large wiggly tumor growing out of my side. I couldn't get rid of the Velcro kid.

Year after year, at the Ranch, we had love-parched boys and girls simply maul Sandy and the nurse, soaking up love from these mother substitutes. A camp nurse injects more love into campers than all of the other medicines combined. Our culture is raising a generation of love-starved children.

The following comments attest the importance of love:

A child is the most needy person in society and his greatest need is love (Dr. Ross Campbell, *How to Really Love Your Child* [Wheaton, Ill.: 1979], 12).

In working with persons who have mental and emotional disturbances, there is one trait which pervades most, if not all, of those seen in the counseling office. This trait is characterized by an incapability to give or receive love and is usually traceable to a person's childhood and parents who have the same problem (Charles Solomon, *The Ins and Outs of Rejection* [Denver, Colo.: Heritage House Publications, 1976], 13).

Dad the Family Encourager must master the techniques to transfer love to his children. This chapter provides five coaching techniques on how to make your children feel loved. The way a father transfers love to his children is to:

1. Speak each child's love language.
2. Show acceptance on a nonperformance basis.
3. Spend time with his children.
4. Demonstrate affection to his children.
5. Get involved in his child's discipline.

SPEAK EACH CHILD'S LOVE LANGUAGE

When Helen used her guinea pigs to communicate love to me, I gained valuable insight into her love language. I began telling her that I loved her ten thousand guinea pigs worth, and even today, we tenderly remind each other of our "piglet" kind of love.

Each of your children has an individual unique love language that is as distinctive and personal as fingerprints. We all have words, phrases, or actions that communicate love in a special way. We use this love language to both give and receive love.

Do you know each of your children's unique love language? Of course you love them, but how much of your love do they perceive? Are you speaking a love language that *means* love to them? Are they receiving the kind of love signals that makes them feel significant? One child explained how she knew Mom loved Dad: "I know Mom loves Dad because she lets him eat cookies anytime he wants to!" The child speaks chocolate chip love.

If you love your children and don't know their love language, they will find it difficult to perceive and experience your love, no matter how great it is nor how many other ways you express it. Love must be transferred in ways that they can understand and identify. They may even erroneously conclude that you don't love them at all just as I concluded about my dad's love for me.

A child desperately needs to perceive love in order to develop healthy self-esteem.

What good does love do if it stays trapped in a lover's heart and is never received by the one loved? Love must be demonstrated or translated into love language that can easily be received to be pragmatic and effective.

Helen and I still communicate with a special love language. She stayed out of college one year to work in the home office of Trammel Crow Construction Company in Dallas. Whenever I flew to the West Coast, I tried to plan a short layover in Dallas to meet Helen at the airport for a brief time together. The first time I met her, I walked into the gate waiting area and saw Helen standing there waiting for me with a *Wall Street Journal* and a chocolate bar. These gifts shouted love to me. I knew that on the way to the airport, Helen had started thinking about me with great affection. As she thought about me on her way to meet me, she reminisced about her childhood and recalled memories of growing up and watching me reading the editorial page of the *Journal* and eating Hershey bars. Because she felt love churning in her heart, she pulled into a convenience store and bought me a *Journal* and some chocolate. She wanted to speak my love language.

I have a little deal with Helen. Every year or so, I buy her a pair of jogging shoes. This gift is my way of making her feel my love in a special way. Every time she puts them on and goes for a little jog, she thinks about me and feels a little shot of love pump through her heart.

How I wish that my dad and I had learned each other's love language. For instance, Dad would have been speaking my love language if he had:

1. Occasionally congratulated me on a job well done.
2. Put his arm around me or let me sit on his lap.
3. Read stories to me or told me stories.
4. Let me borrow the car more than once a semester.
5. Invited me to go fishing in the officers' PT boat with him while we lived in Alaska.

I now know that Dad loved me, but I missed all the signals when I was growing up. Dad and I didn't learn to love each other and communicate it until the last three years of his life when we finally began to speak each other's love language. How sad we waited so long.

Don't you wait. Get going now. You need to learn the unique details of your child's love language as soon as possible. Men, make your child's love language your mother tongue.

SHOW ACCEPTANCE ON
A NONPERFORMANCE BASIS

When we returned from a family European speaking tour back in 1983, Helen (sixteen years old) approached me with great apprehension. She had lost her camera and had fretted about telling me for weeks. She finally blurted it out and stood bravely for my reaction.

I understand Helen. She is exactly like me. We are the absent-minded professor types. I have lost enough merchandise to fill a football field. I have lost coats, ties, shoes, bikes, toys, firearms, tons of sporting equipment, people, trucks, towns, horses, ranches, and houses. If one can own it, I can lose it. My college roommate, John Battle, says, "There is a giant warehouse in the sky filled to the brim with things that Dave Simmons has lost, and they will be restored only at the Rapture when he bumps into them on the way up."

So I understand Helen. She has a "bent" I know well. I know how she feels about the loss. I know the injury to her self-esteem from losing it. I also know she needs to learn to be more careful and can learn better habits that can cut down, but not eliminate, her losses.

With this understanding in mind, I knew nothing I did would bring back her camera or motivate her to do better. She was already totally committed to improving in this area, but she was working against her "bent." The best thing I could do was encourage her and let her know that I loved her and would not let anything come between us.

Therefore, I merely expressed regret for her loss of her pictures on the film in the camera, encouraged her to be more careful, and discussed ways she could earn money to buy an inexpensive camera. She flung herself on me, gave me a big hug, and said, "Guess what? Dad, you're great! I love you so much!" She felt good because my love, kindness, and consideration did not go up and down with her performance. She knew she was loved. She never got the impression that things were more important to me than her.

Acceptance on a nonperformance basis is essential for teens. When the teen perceives that acceptance comes with performance, the whole contract changes. You revert back into natural human love and automatically set up the win/lose trap.

Brandon's first summer in Little League baseball was a disaster. Because of his birth date, it worked out that he was a year younger than the youngest of the other players. He went the entire season without a hit. I mean, he batted .000. I died the death of a thousand strikes. Game after game, he approached the plate and failed. How can you accept a kid like that?

You would think a pitch would accidentally hit the bat at least once. He couldn't even get a walk. Not only did he fail but it also didn't seem to bother him too much. That made me madder. Champions get hits, and they suffer anguish if they don't.

No one will ever know how I suffered. Can you imagine my embarrassment when my boy came to bat and the coach rolled his eyes, the players slumped back on the bench, and the parents groaned. The reason for my pain lies in the tendency of fathers to live their lives through their children. It was me coming to bat. It was me watching called strikes. It was me letting the team down.

My typical reaction was to shift into the Little League Angry Father Syndrome that turns Little League ball parks into the killing fields of America. I got mad at Brandon, my alter self. I wanted to yell instructions at him. Encourage him. Bribe him. Threaten him. Then, when he failed, I wanted to punish him. Disassociate from him. Withdraw. Whose boy is this? He couldn't be mine.

Those were my natural inclinations, but I bucked them and applied the principles of unconditional love and bonding that I had been studying. It took everything I had to override my emotions and disassociate my feelings about baseball and consider Brandon separately as a person. There is no question that I love Brandon, but in certain situations, I lose my context, and my emotions take over. I am temporarily deceived (insane?), and my values get turned upside down.

With hard work, I overcame my emotions and kept my values and priorities right. I loved him unconditionally, and I showed it. I hugged him after every game and held his hand on the way to the car. I told him, "Brandon, son, I love you. I'm proud of your perseverance and bravery in the face of defeat. You are a real champion to endure the frustration, to keep trying and not give up. You are the kind of man I would always want on my team" (along with seven sluggers).

It was hard, not because I didn't love him—I deeply loved him, but my emotions did not feel at all like loving and accepting him. It was a case of ignoring my emotions and speaking what I *knew*, not what I *felt*. I knew that the father-son relationship hung by a slender thread, and if I rejected him during those times, it would have snapped, and he would have separated himself from me. I might have lost him.

To me, our relationship was far more important than his batting average. Brandon is now twenty years old, and we are great friends. What do you think had the greatest impact on our present relationship, his batting average that year or the way I responded to him?

These incidents illustrate a major key to loving. Successful loving occurs only when people practice a policy of "total acceptance" toward one another. People must reach the level of commitment to one another where they all have confidence that they accept each other on a nonperformance basis. In Volume 3, *Dad the Family Mentor*, I explain the tension between discipline, correction, and nonperformance love.

Helen and Brandon have total confidence that Sandy and I accept them without any conditions. They are absolutely positive that there is nothing that they could ever do or anything that could ever happen to them that would stop our love for them. They are doomed to unconditional love so they might as well learn to put up with it. This kind of love is why our family is so close despite the many mistakes I made and the way I was so much of the time when they were young.

When I talk about accepting children, I mean doing whatever it takes to make them *feel* like you accept their total person — personhood, personality, and feelings. If you deny these things, they will feel rejected. You, who know them best, must accept them as total persons.

Looking at it from a negative view, how much pain do you suppose children feel when those who know them the best reject them the most? Never underestimate your power to hurt your children and destroy their feelings of significance and value.

SPEND TIME WITH YOUR CHILDREN

When you, the male dominant authority figure, give your time to a child, you generate great feelings of love and significance in the child's heart. A child thinks, "If Dad loves me, he will spend time with me," and "I feel significant when Dad spends time with me." Time is a love language term that all children understand. (Your wife does too.)

It doesn't take long for a child to realize that you consider time to be your most important resource. They see how you hoard and protect your discretionary time. When you spend time with them, they pick up on the transfer of its value. You tell them that they are as important as your time.

Yet, what kind of stats are American men compiling? One study by an Ivy League university revealed that fathers spend an average of thirty-seven seconds a day in meaningful transaction with their infants. The average father spends less than twenty minutes per week in meaningful conversation with his teenager. If you don't spend time with your children, they remain unconvinced of your love, regardless of your words.

Give Quality Time

Each child has a father-shaped vacuum in his or her heart, which no one can fill—except his or her dad. When children thirst for their dad, nothing else will satisfy. Only a long quenching drink of their dad will suffice. You better be there to quench their dad-thirst. If you don't satisfy them, the next time they will be a little longer coming and a little quicker going.

Why do small children repeatedly ask you the same silly questions? They know the answers. Why do they want you to read the same old stories time after time? They have them memorized. Change one of the stories, and you will be instantly corrected.

More than the answers and stories, they want *you*. They want to be held by your muscled arms, hear your deep voice, and be held against your hairy chest. The questions and stories are merely their little techniques to be with you. They want you to step into their hearts, into their lives, and be a part of them.

Give a Quantity of Time

By the way, don't fall for the old quality versus quantity myth. Many believe: "Well, I may not spend a vast quantity of time with my children, but when I do, I make sure it is quality time." This reasoning fails to consider that quality time with children cannot be programmed; children do not regulate their teachability and responsiveness according to your schedule.

Can you imagine me making this statement to Helen when she was five years old? "OK, Helen, next Wednesday at 6:42, I've scheduled seventeen valuable minutes to spend quality time with you. We're gonna have a good time! Now, set your watch. Be there! Be ready!"

No. You must spend a vast quantity of time with a child in order to seize those special brief moments when the child turns to you with wide-eyed wonder and grasps intensely for heart-to-heart intimacy. They are like little birds in the nest waiting and waiting and then, suddenly, their bony heads shoot up, their cavernous beaks pop open, and they want the worm, *right now!* They desperately want a drink of Dad.

You cannot give quality time unless you give a quantity of time. You just have to hang around. You need to be there. Be alert for those priceless irreplaceable moments when your child needs to belt down a strong gulp of Dad.

To be honest, most of the time you spend with your child will be wasted. Not much of it will be productive. They won't sit there and lap you up for two straight hours. What they do is suddenly—no one can predict when—spin around, open up, and take a long swig of Dad. The little hole in the window opens up and lets you in. Then they shut it, go back to their preoccupation, and put you in a holding mode again. This means you have to waste a quantity of time to get the quality time. You just have to hang around.

Another common excuse is "I don't have control over my schedule so I can't spend a quantity of time with my children."

In a national men's survey, I asked the question, "What is the number one obstacle keeping you from being the family shepherd you really want to be?" What do you think their answer was? Ninety-five percent of the men answered: "Time." Men claim they are too busy. They are dramatically overscheduled.

It may be true that they are overscheduled and exhausted. But this reason is still a cop-out. It's not a question of time. A man does what he wants to do. His busy schedule reveals his priorities, not his unavailability. It's a decision problem, not a chronology problem. A man decides what goes into his schedule. He chooses his top priorities and makes sure they get scheduled.

What if you are a doctor on call all the time? What if you are a sales rep and travel all the time? What if you are trying to get your small business over the hump? What if you coach, do shift work, police work, or anything that keeps you from quenching your child's father thirst?.

Then, you face choices. No one *makes* you do anything in North America (except pay taxes). You are free to sell your labor in a free market and make a living *for* your children—and *with* your children. Even if you spent ten hard years preparing for your practice or career, you are not predestined to lock yourself up and doom your children.

Is any career worth the life of your child? Are any career goals or sales quotas worth your child? When I put it this way, of course not. The problem, however, is that men don't see their choice in such stark black-and-white terms. They see a light gray choice, "For a while, don't you see; just until . . . " They never notice that light gray always darkens gradually until they have slipped into black and can no longer see the child.

Neglect happens. Passive indifference is a creeper. Only intense vigilance keeps job chauvinism at bay. No father says, "Well, today I decide! Is it gonna be my job or my kid?" The subtle lie is, "I don't have to choose. I can have it all if I play my cards right. I can double up here and cut short there and juggle the rest."

By the way, don't think your job really cares. It is not a sentient being with interest in and compassion for you. You fill a box on some chart somewhere, and you are extremely replaceable. After my dad died, I went to his office and gathered his belongings in a small box from another man already sitting at his desk. My mother's personal effects fit into a cigar box, and they didn't miss her a single day after she died.

After I die, I want my personal effects to be found in the hearts of my children, not in a cigar box. I want to clock out in my kids. I am not an organizational box to them. No one on the face of the earth can fill my shoes as the father of Helen and Brandon. Why remove myself from a job fit only for me to fill a job anyone can fit into?

My advice, men, is save your children. The world is full of fathers who will sell out their family for bucks and booty. Well, let them. Let the dead bury the dead. But, not you. A holy calling and ordination summons you to practice the profession of fatherhood.

You may find yourself in an awkward position. You know your job causes you to sacrifice your children, but you don't want to admit it. If you did, you might have to make some decisions. You may decide to stay where you are and play Russian roulette with the lives of your children. You may decide to quit and find another job. Maybe ask for a transfer. Maybe refuse a transfer or promotion. Sir, with all respect to you and your career, please see the truth and do what you must do to honor your children. Decide yes to give yourself to your children. Let your career serve your children, not you.

DEMONSTRATE AFFECTION
TO YOUR CHILDREN

Many children are getting shortchanged on affection as evidenced by a recent survey that asked children to compare their dads with the TV. Over half of the tested children indicated that they liked the

TV better than their dads. Why? Because the TV was always "there," and their dads weren't. The TV did not promise affection and renege; it made modest promises and kept them. The TV affirmed them by making them feel significant; they could control it and keep it from "going away."

Don't force your kids to squeeze affection from the boob tube. Kids measure affection from their dads on a Richter scale. Nobody can cause a child's heart to quake with affection quite like Dad. Picture the ecstatic look on your child's face when you shoot him a dose of straight love.

Children have an affection jug that must be kept filled, or they will fill it with poison. As Dad the Family Nurturer, you need to keep that jug filled. If you do, children will soon learn to keep their jug filled by themselves. If you don't, they will feel a chronic emptiness and spend the rest of their lives frantically searching for outlets of affection. Their capacity to feel affection will be injured.

This section will cover five ways you can show affection to your children: Give them biblical truth, yourself, your ears, verbal, and nonverbal signals.

Give Your Children Biblical Truth
In 1 Thessalonians 2:8, the Bible gives two good suggestions on how to show affection: "Having thus a fond affection for you, we were well pleased to impart to you not only the Gospel but also our own lives, because you had become very dear to us."

When you have fond affection, you are concerned about a person's spirit and their eternal condition. Affection calls for a spiritual relationship and the discussion of how to become a Christian and how to grow to maturity in Christ (see chap. 5). As Dad the Family Priest, you show affection when you minister to your child.

Give Your Children Your Life
Showing affection means imparting your own self. You need to give your child your self. A form of giving your self is giving attention. For a child, attention is an odd commodity. The more you give, the less they need. The less you give, the more they demand, and they will stop at nothing to get it.

Unfortunately, when a child has a strong healthy need for attention and tries to get it, many parents react by rationing it or withholding it completely. Perhaps they suspect the child will develop an addiction, or maybe they don't want the child to control them. In any case, parents should not ration or withhold their attention, which is the same thing as their lives, to their children.

Listen to Your Children

Listening is one form of attention. Mick Yoder, my close friend and an excellent family shepherd, drove down the street with one of his four sons, Benji, who was in the front seat with him. Benji rattled on and on about little boy topics while Mick, lost in thought, gave a token nod now and then. Benji noticed his lack of attention and said, "Dad ... Dad ... DAAAAD!" After Mick gave another indifferent nod, Benji jumped up in front of his dad's face, blocked the view of the busy street, grabbed his dad's ears with both hands, and hollered, "Dad, listen to me when I talk to you!"

In love language, listening means: "I love you and choose to give the gift of listening (self) for your benefit." Listening is love in action. When you listen, you are saying, "Because you are extremely significant, I consider listening to you the most important thing I can do."

How would you feel if the President of the United States called you on the phone (with the Prime Minister of Russia at the end of another line) to get your feelings and input on an emergency problem with the Soviets? Listening builds significance. The more important the listener, the more significant the talker feels. When a father, a dominant male authority figure, carefully listens to his child, he or she feels deeply significant.

On the other hand, when a father does not listen, the child feels the intense pain of rejection. A child can even feel sharp pangs of false guilt and feel like a nonperson.

The sad thing about this situation is that most parents do not even realize that poor communication hurts their children. One recent survey showed that 79 percent of interviewed parents thought they had communicated well with their children. Their children, however, had a different response: 81 percent said their parents did not communicate well with them.

Your children measure your love by how much of your inner self you are willing to deposit into them. They don't want your words, gifts, and toys; they want you. Oh, they will temporarily settle for the sparkle and glitter we bribe them with, but they soon realize these things are diversions, and their thirst for the real *you* continues to build.

Teenagers, especially, recognize when parents are buying them off. True, they love the credit cards, the expensive clothes, and fancy cars, but at the same time, they deeply resent parents who hide behind things. They might not admit it, but they do.

Give Your Children Verbal Signals
A strong father communicates affection verbally. He knows that kids need to hear love expressed directly, plainly, and clearly. Here are some verbal techniques:

● Tell them, "I love you" and "I appreciate you" frequently. Try to give specific reasons. The details mean a lot and make your comments more believable.
● Compliment and brag about them constantly. Focus your remarks on their mental, emotional, and spiritual assets. Commend their achievements, but be wary that they don't sense a love earned by their performance. Avoid praising their physical looks and beauty. If they are attractive, they will know it. You want to emphasize their inner person.
● Say nice things about them when they are not present, but you know either they are near enough that they can hear you or they will hear about it later.

Give Your Children Nonverbal Signals of Love
Strong fathers pay attention to their children and soon learn to transfer love in a variety of nonverbal ways. Incidentally, children believe your nonverbal actions far more than your words. Try some of these techniques.

● Touch and hug each child every day. You cannot overdo physical attention. Don't worry about overstimulating your daughter or awakening homosexual tendencies in your son. In fact, a physically affectionate father produces chaste daughters and manly sons. Of course, never, never be sexually inappropriate.

Lots of fatherly physical affection satisfies their deep needs, and they will develop a healthy physical attitude. If you withhold physical affection from your daughter, she will develop an unhealthy need for it that will get her into trouble when she matures. Paternal deprivation can cause a son to fixate on male attention and seek endorsement from other men. Most homosexuals come from non-

nurturant passive/absent fathers and overbearing mothers.
● Know their schedules and attend their functions. Go to their ball games, dance recitals, and school homerooms.
● Know their friends, teachers, coaches, and other important people in their lives. Sponsor projects with their friends, like slumber parties, lake trips, and parties. They think, "Love me, love my friends."

GET INVOLVED IN CHILD DISCIPLINE

Sandy used to raise collie puppies. We once had a litter of nine collie pups born at King's Arrow Ranch and had to move them to Arkansas when camp was over for the summer. After I took down their fence, they became tense and quiet. They stepped tentatively past the boundary where the fence had stood, then dashed back, diving into a big whimpering pile. They had considered the fence an obstacle to their freedom, but they panicked when they felt the loss of security disappear with the fence.

Discipline acts like the fence. It appears to be a detested limit to the child, but it actually serves as protection. Children without limits develop severe emotional problems because they feel no security. When they grow older and can understand that many of their problems stem from the absence of reasonable limits, they will conclude that their parents did not love them or consider them significant enough to bother with enforcing limits.

Children know you love them if you discipline them. Proverbs 13:24 says, "He who spares his rod hates his son, *but he who loves him disciplines him diligently*" (italics mine).

Contrary to popular opinion, children want limits. They subconsciously know that limits reflect love, care, and concern and that they provide security. Appropriate limits carefully explained and firmly enforced constitute one of the most effective ways to communicate love to children. A child without limits is like a locomotive without tracks; it has no place to go and just sits there building up steam and pressure.

When parents define specific limits and enforce them, they not only build character, but in the process, they also are providing serious attention to the child. Children want attention from you so desperately that they will even deliberately misbehave just to get you to lock your attention onto them. A spanking is a cheap price for a child to pay for the intense concentration that the parent gives during the process.

The Fatherhood Function "To Equip" covers what we refer to as child-raising or child discipline and is a topic worthy of the entire Volume 3, *Dad the Family Mentor.* "To Equip" is a process with the following four steps, each of which has two full chapters in Volume 3.

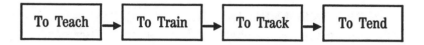

To Teach → To Train → To Track → To Tend

The discipline process seems difficult and unrewarding, but, in the long run, it must be done to yield a life of peace and righteousness. Hebrews 12:11 puts it best: "All discipline for the moment seems not to be joyful, but sorrowful; yet to those who have been trained by it, afterwards it yields the peaceful fruit of righteousness."

If a father loves his children and wants them trained to enjoy life, he will pay the price and do diligent discipline. If he doesn't, he's only saying he doesn't really care. Without discipline, a child foolishly squanders his life away. Proverbs 22:15 says, "Foolishness is bound up in the heart of a child; the rod of discipline will remove it far from him."

THE KANSAS FLATS
These are five ways you can begin to put spiritual love into action and communicate love to your children. Study your child carefully and consult your wife. Your child has little love buttons that need to be pushed, and it's so easy if you just learn them and commit yourself to doing them.

On our annual family ski trip, we drive straight through for twenty hours to ski in Colorado. With the kids now old enough, we each can drive two-hour shifts. A couple of weeks ago on a return trip, Helen drew the 2 A.M. shift. I rode shotgun, and Brandon and Sandy racked out on the bed in the back of the van.

All of a sudden—WHAM, BANG, WHUMP WHUMP WHUMP. Sweet little twenty-two-year-old Helen creamed something, and *both* right tires exploded. There we were in west Kansas on I-70 in the middle of the night in fifteen-degree temperature with two flats and only one spare.

Words cannot express how Helen felt. The fatigue of late-night driving, the trauma of slamming into something and ripping open the tires, and the apprehension about how Dad would react had her in a delicate state. The wrong move on my part would have caused her to withdraw and isolate herself.

My natural reaction to incidents like this one is to get angry, personalize it, and blame somebody. If I had attacked Helen at that point, however, it would have caused a rupture in the togetherness feelings we had built during the vacation.

Scrambling out of a fitful sleep into that situation did not activate all my love and affection switches, but I ignored all my natural responses. Instead, I immediately reached over, hugged her, and told Helen, "It's OK. It could have happened to anyone. You did great just keeping us on the road. Don't worry about it."

When I awoke fully and realized the situation we were in, I casually informed her that she was disinherited. (Just kidding.) I spent a lot of time assuring her that everything was OK. No big deal.

Helen deeply regretted the accident, but she felt secure in her relationship with me. She rested in the grace that came with my unconditional acceptance and approval of her. She knew I hated the accident and the trouble it caused, but she also knew that my negative feelings were directed elsewhere and not at her.

E-TEAM HUDDLE GUIDE
CHAPTER ONE:
DAD THE FAMILY ENCOURAGER

E-TEAM REVIEW
10–15 minutes

Dad, the Family Shepherd
E-TEAM

After coffee and fellowship, allow each dad to cover the following:
1. Tell the E-Team your name, occupation, and phone number.
2. Tell the E-Team your wife's name and the names and ages of your children. Record their family information below.

Team Member	His Wife	Phone	Children
1. _____	_____	Of_____ Ho_____	_____
2. _____	_____	Of_____ Ho_____	_____
3. _____	_____	Of_____ Ho_____	_____
4. _____	_____	Of_____ Ho_____	_____
5. _____	_____	Of_____ Ho_____	_____
6. _____	_____	Of_____ Ho_____	_____

E-TEAM DISCUSSION
50–60 minutes

This part allows you to discuss the key concepts in this chapter and relate them to your individual lives. Be sure to leave time to complete the workout and encouragement sections.

THE PRINCIPLES (Check the text for help.)
1. What are the five methods of helping a child feel a father's love?
2. Which one do you think is most important? Why?

THE IMPLICATIONS (Why are these ideas significant?)
3. Take each method and discuss the effect of its omission.
4. Which of these five methods do you think are most neglected?

THE APPLICATION (How do these ideas affect me?)
5. Which method did your father do best and least with you.
6. Tell the E-Team which method you do best and which one you need to work on the most.
7. Tell the E-Team the love language of each child in your family.

E-TEAM WORKOUT
10–15 minutes

Allow each dad to choose one of the project options (plays) to perform during the week. If desired, design your own project.

1st PLAY:
Make an appointment with your wife and discuss the five love methods. Ask her which ones she received as a child and which ones she did not receive. Ask her how she feels about it.

2nd PLAY:
Discuss the five love methods with your wife. Evaluate the love that each child feels. Talk about the love language of each child.

3rd PLAY:
Talk to God about your track record of showing love. Ask Him to help you in this area of fatherhood. Write out a list of ways you will show love to each child and your wife this week. Then, go do it.

E-TEAM ENCOURAGEMENT
5–10 minutes

Close the meeting in prayer. Include in your prayer a specific request for spiritual power to complete your project successfully.

BREAK THE HUDDLE, GO HOME AND RUN THE PLAY!

Chapter Two
Dad the Family
Peacemaker

*"It wasn't until somewhere in my fortieth year that
I began to connect the problem with my dad to the
problem with my sons."*
— Dr. Charles Sell

THE FOX HUNT

In the middle of a cold winter night, my dad crept quietly into the living room where a half-dozen children were sleeping on the floor and woke me. He cautioned me to stealth as we bundled up in our heavy winter gear and slipped quietly out of the house. I had no idea what was going on.

The Major Amos E. Simmons family had just finished two years in Alaska and were visiting the Simmons clan in Tangipahoa Parish in Louisiana before reporting to Ft. Bliss in El Paso, Texas. I was fifteen years old and had been sleeping under downy blankets with my cousins when Dad mysteriously abducted me.

Dad put me in a beat-up old step-side pickup with a cold metal dashboard and no insulation. He pulled the choke and revved the cranky engine over a few times. It didn't catch. He sat back, paused, and watched me with an odd look in his eye while his cold breath puffed out clouds, fogging the windows. He tried again. Sucking the last of the juice from the cold battery, the old Ford finally fired.

Dad shifted to neutral, let off the clutch, got out of the shuddering truck, and started loading some bulky shapes into the back. I couldn't see who it was, but he was mumbling and grunting as if talking to someone. He got back in, twisted around, peered through the cab back window between the mounted rifles, and yelled a muffled directive of some kind.

Then, we eased down the gravel road to the highway and drove several miles until we picked up an old logging road. We turned east onto it, went through a cutover, passed a stand of long-leaf yellow pine, and pulled up to a little clearing that held five other rust-splotched pickups.

By the light of the full moon, I could see whiskered dark shapes huddled together. Men were gathering. I could see dots of cigarette glow and hear the gruff muffled talk of men among men. A jug made rounds. A few were packing their first tobacco chews. The musky aroma of thick chickory coffee escaped from a thermos bottle.

After a short wait, the men huddled together and became quiet in order to hear the softly spoken words of my grandpa. Then, they got started. They each went to the bed of his own pickup, and with much fumbling in the dark and banging of tailgates, they set loose the dogs.

These excited dogs burst forth from their cages in a frothy frenzy. They whipped around with mouths slobbering, noses smelling, and wide eyes gaping whitely in the dark as they anticipated the hunt, run, and kill. The men's coarse shouts and shrill whistling fell away as the pack of hounds bunched up and moved out like a large churning, grumbling shadow.

From within the truck cab, I gazed with fascination on my first fox hunt.

The men clumped up to the tailgate of a pickup and did what fox hunters do—they listened. A fox hunter doesn't follow the dogs, and he doesn't shoot foxes. He doesn't talk to his buddies or build noisy, crackling fires to stay warm. He does absolutely nothing except stand, freeze, and listen. Your top-grade fox hunters can lean against the pickup for hours in subzero weather without making a move.

They stand there and listen to the dogs howl through the woods chasing after one horrified fox. And they think, "There goes Ole Ruby down to Widow Johnson's place. Listen to Ole Blue! He's out in front and sounds like he's a-chasin' a red fox. Man, Ole Jake's got a good mouth on him. Poor Ole Bella, she cain't run no more." Then, they mentally record these impressions for playback should they chance to meet one another later in the week.

The John Wayne Fathers

I sulked in the truck, too cold to sleep and too bored to stay awake. The last thing on my fun list was listening to dogs yap through the forest. I thought, "I wonder why Dad did this to me? Why does he have to make me so miserable? Dad never thinks of me and what I like—only what he wants."

Actually, this episode was one of the most significant of my life. It was Dad's way of telling me that he loved me and accepted me as a man. He was bringing me into the fellowship of the men of the clan. Nobody, but nobody, went fox hunting with the men—it was the esteemed inner circle of the tribe, the elite. Dad was announcing that he loved me and accepted me as a man. This experience was my rite of passage, and I missed it.

It wasn't Dad's style to explain this episode to me. He never told me he loved me in ways I understood until I was thirty-something. He probably didn't know the term, "rite of passage": he just felt it was time, and when it's time, you do it—you don't talk about it. He loved me, but it never occurred to him it would be good to say, "Dave, I love you." He clothed me, fed me, put me through school, and took me on the Fox Hunt. What else is there?

Here is a perfect example of a father demonstrating love and respect for his son, and his son not picking it up. I thought Dad did not love me. For the first thirty years of my life, I wondered why he hated me so much. It seemed as if he had a low-grade smoldering dislike for me that often, unpredictably, flared up to singe my soul and sear my heart.

Now, I look back and realize that my dad did not loathe me; he loved me. I know he loved me because everytime I walked around town, everyone would come up to me and tell me all about myself and how proud my dad was of me. Dad bragged so much about "his boy" that everyone knew all about my football career and my ministry. Dad could tell anyone else how much he loved me, even a stranger, but I never heard it.

Even though Dad's love existed, it never touched me. He just didn't know how to communicate his love to me. He could not speak my love language, and I couldn't interpret his. I could read his anger and disappointment like a book, but he kept his love for me hidden. Love in the wrong language remains love unsavored. To a child, love that is untranslated feels the same as no love at all. It also causes just as much heart damage.

Dad's generation, the World War II Warrior Dads, took up the strong, silent John Wayne role. Their manly code of conduct prohibited them from showing affection to their sons. The John Wayne generation locked into their own macho love language.

These baby boomer fathers seemed to have had a deep-seated fear that if you brought love, affection, and emotion into the father/son equation, you were just asking for your boy to deviate into a homosexual. Little did they realize that appropriate love and affection for a son is the greatest insurance for healthy gender role preference, adoption, and affiliation.

Boys with a strong father's love develop deep security in their male identity. Many boys without a father's love struggle with masculinity and pursue perverted liaisons with other men (father-simulators) to compensate for their loss. Also, many girls get confused about their femininity when a father's love is absent. Nothing validates and secures a girl's healthy feelings about her womanhood more than the affirmation that comes from a nurturing father.

LOVE QUENCHED

Before a father can provide his children with the love they crave, he must have his own love thirst quenched. A man desperately seeking love can't pour out what he doesn't have. His pain keeps him in the receiving mode, and he can't muster the emotional and psychological energy to be in a transmitting mode.

To pour love out for others, a father must dry out his pain pool (as described in Volume 1: Dad the Family Coach) and fill up his love lake. Most of the time, this pain in a man comes from an unhealthy relationship he had with his father.

A man has to go back and establish peace and a love relationship with his father before he can crash through the barriers to his own children and give them the love they need. If a father intends to perform the Fatherhood Function "To Love," he must clear the deck from his past and get his heart in shape to transfer love.

If he suffers in a dysfunctional relationship with his father, he remains emotionally and psychologically trapped, and he is not free to release himself fully to his own family. Many men need to make peace with their fathers before they can allow love to flow freely through them to their families.

This brings up two sets of crucial questions:

First question:
How bad does your relationship with your dad have to be before you seek healing? How can you tell if you need this healing?

The answer:

No father/child relationship is perfect, and into the life of every child a little pain must fall. You may not need massive healing, but all men need to do some repair work.

Second question:

How important is your dad's cooperation in the process? What if he refuses or is incapable of participation? What if he is dead, you have never known him, or you can't find him?

The answer:

It would be great if you and your dad could work through this process together, but if you can't, you still need to go through the process because you have a pain pool in your heart and you must and can be healed. The healing comes when God takes your heart through the process, and your dad does not have to be present for God to mend your heart and drain your pain pool.

There is no quick-fix formula for establishing peace with your dad because every father/child relationship is incredibly unique with peculiar variables and is in a constant state of flux. The process for healing is both an art and a skill. As an art, it takes a sensitive touch and sense of balance, timing, and empathy to employ the principles. As a skill, it requires a process that is both sequential and cyclical: There are phases and steps to follow but there is much backtracking, repeating, spurting, and stopping. It's more like a dance than a hike.

The process I recommend has these elements:

1. Take responsibility for your own life.
2. Achieve peace with the Heavenly Father.
3. Face reality: Identify the pain.
4. Grieve for your losses.
5. Confess your parts of the problem.
6. Forgive your father.
7. Put love into action.

Unfortunately, not knowing these principles, I blindly struggled through the healing process and managed to stretch it out over thirteen years. Further complications arose when my dad died three years into the restoration process. I had to continue the healing process without my dad and am still working through it today.

One final point: This chapter deals with how negative father power has adversely affected you and what you can do to overcome it. As you read this chapter, realize that in order to keep your children from having to go through a healing process like this in years to come, you need to dedicate yourself to performing the Fatherhood Function "To Love" like a champion.

TAKE RESPONSIBILITY FOR YOUR OWN LIFE

If you had a difficult dad, one of the worst things you can do is to continue to blame your dad for all your present problems. Dwelling on past injustices has little to do with your recovering for future accomplishments. As long as you stay locked into a blame mode, you allow the past to control and manipulate you.

You can't change the way your father related to you as a child. But, you can change the future that your old past was headed for. You can switch futures by taking responsibility for your own life and doing whatever is required to be healed and make a fresh beginning.

If you focus on the past and the damage you sustained, you can actually develop an addiction for feeling sorry for yourself, and you will increase your discouragement. The more discouraged you are, the more immobilized you become (discourage means "let your hands go slack"). The feelings of depression and futility that accompany being obsessed with your misfortune takes away hope, and we need hope to give us excitement and purpose for the future. God tells us in Jeremiah 29:11: " 'For I know the plans that I have for you,' declares the Lord, 'plans for welfare and not for calamity to give you a future and a hope.' "

If you suffer from the impact of a dysfunctional family, you need to face reality, quit blaming others, take control of your life, and take the proper steps for recovery. No one else can walk the path to healing for you. If you don't do it, you have no hope.

ACHIEVE PEACE
WITH THE HEAVENLY FATHER

Hope comes from God. He can solve all our dysfunctional family problems and heal all our pain. He can fill in our gaps and make us whole, well-balanced people. Hope and peace require that a man drink from the springs of living water, Jesus Christ. No man can attain the type of spiritual love that his family needs unless he has peace with God through Jesus Christ (see chap. 3 in Dad the *Family Coach*). When we know God, He abides in us and enables us to spray His love on those around us. In 1 John 4:7-12, 16, John tells us where spiritual love comes from and how it works through us:

> Beloved, let us love one another, for love is from God; and every one who loves is born of God and knows God. The one who does not love does not know God, for God is love. By this the love of God was manifested in us, that God has sent His only begotten Son into the world so that we might live through Him. In this is love, not that we loved God, but that He loved us and sent His Son to be the propitiation for our sins. Beloved, if God so loved us, we also ought to love one another. No one has beheld God at any time; if we love one another, God abides in us, and His love is perfected in us. . . . And we have come to know and have believed the love which God has for us. God is love, and the one who abides in love abides in God, and God abides in him.

This passage tells us that when we become Christians, God, who is love, starts living inside us and loving others through us. In fact, this new type of love is "Exhibit A," which proves that we have entered into eternal life with Christ. The best way to get a glimpse of God is to witness His love working among His children. The best way to maximize love in your family is to abide in God.

If you haven't already, I challenge you men to trust Christ as your Lord and Savior and begin tapping into His source of divine love. Walk in His Spirit by faith and let His love fill you.

God deals with us directly, but we also need others to act as channels through whom He can minister to us. The New Testament is filled with admonition for us to confess our sins to one another and bear one another's burdens, and to meet together to encourage, confront, and heal one another. What better arena to process in than with an E-Team.

Some of us may need professional help. For a free assessment of the degree of your trouble, contact RAPHA, a national chain of Christian counseling centers.

FACE REALITY: IDENTIFY THE PAIN

For many years, I felt confused and wondered why I seemed to be so different from others. I didn't seem to be able to develop close friendships. I thought it was because I was an army brat and had to move all the time. I was a troubled young man, however, and I didn't know it. I lived in unreality. In trying to cope with the pain from my dad, I had set up a failure system that kept me from seeing the truth and making healthy corrections.

Pain Happens

I did not know that I desperately needed to find peace with Dad because I was not in touch with the pain caused by our relationship. In actuality, the pain was so terrible that I had established an elaborate system of hiding it, and it was this protection system that kept causing me severe emotional damage and disrupted my relationships.

You can hide pain but you can't stop its effects. It mutates into rage, anger, hostility, and bitterness. It makes you hard to live with. As a result, I became touchy and temperamental. Little things triggered big reactions. The more people got to know me, the more they backed away. I reacted with denial and blame—I denied my own problems and blamed others.

I did not see or live in reality. I was headed for disaster. This process chart pictures the destructive cycle in my life:

The Father/Pain/Enmity Cycle

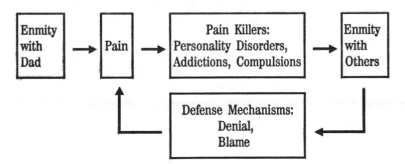

Many of my difficulties in life originated from my painful relationship with Dad. To get long-range permanent healing, I had to get right with him, but I could not see this problem because I had buried the pain and couldn't trace my other problems back to the root cause. To break the cycle, I needed to surface the pain and remove it in order to eliminate the need for the problem-causing pain killers.

Surfacing pain may not seem like a good idea, but it is essential. When we experienced pain as a child, we did not handle it properly, allowing it to handicap us. Now, as adults, we need to bring up the pain, take a second shot at it, and blow it out of our system.

Useful Pain

Though pain happens, it is a useful tool. Even though pain hurts, it is not a bad thing because it produces positive results. Pain is a God-given asset that does two things:
1. It tells us when we are sustaining damage.
2. It identifies the source of damage.

Without pain, we wouldn't realize how bad things are, and we wouldn't know where to go to solve the problem. The worst thing you can do is hide or ignore the pain. Not dealing with the pain allows the problem to go unchecked and the injury to increase. Pain must be dealt with; it needs to be thrown out, not covered up.

Damaging Pain

Obviously, when we were children, we did not know sophisticated methods of conflict resolution. Nevertheless, we survived with whatever worked to bury the pain which a dysfunctional father caused with his father power. Some children get quiet and retreat; some get hyper and aggressive. A child with excessive pain often overfixates on diversionary things that lead to addictions, obsessions, and compulsions. Whatever it is, it numbs the pain.

These techniques, however, only cover the pain. The pain flows underground to fill a large reservoir, a pain pool. The greater the pain, the deeper we bury it and the harder it is to get in touch with it later. This father-pain lives in the heart of many men (and women) today. Until they get in touch with it and process it out of their lives, they will continue to spin around in the pain/blame cycle.

Identified Pain

Ironically, people who suffer most from the pain usually project the image of being tough, hard-nosed, crusty, and impervious to hurt. They would be the last to recognize their own pain and sensitivity to hurt. They do not see their pain because they deny their problems. They live in an unreal world and can't explain why they continue to have bad feelings and disrupted relationships.

After years of reinforcing the Father/Pain/Enmity Cycle, it's difficult to see the connection between father-pain and broken relationships. When father-pain is invisible, people are limited in their recovery efforts. They plaster cosmetics over their problems instead of going back to process the pain and making peace with their fathers.

Sometimes it's hard for you to tell if you need to make peace with your dad by merely looking at him. To your mind, a dysfunctional dad can appear OK because of the fantasy bond. Also, maybe you haven't seen a nurturing father with which to compare him.

Your father may be covert in his dysfunction; that is, his symptoms are hidden from you, but your heart still takes a pounding. He may be a compulsive gambler, a sex addict, a spendaholic, a thrill addict, or a workaholic. He may be able to keep his dysfunction out of your sight, but he can't hide his heart, which causes your heart the greatest problems.

Your pain pool can fill up even when your dad is not ranting, raving, and abusing. The sins of omission are just as devastating. When he neglects you, ignores you, abandons you, or excludes you, your pain pool may be tranquil on the surface but quietly be rising and can eventually reach the flood stage.

Trying to determine your father-pain by reading your father or looking for raw pain can be deceptive. You may need to examine other areas of your life and see if they point to the father-pain root cause. Here is a short list of common symptoms of father-pain:

1. We believe no one loves or respects us.
2. We feel tense, anxious, and apprehensive.
3. We have addictions, obsessions, and compulsions.
4. We lose our temper and feel extremely hostile.
5. We insist on controlling others.
6. We make others constantly prove their love for us.
7. We try to present a perfect image of success.
8. We act in ways we don't want to and can't stop.
9. We feel alone, isolated, and abandoned.
10. We are never satisfied, gratified, or content.
11. We think we must be perfect to gain approval.
12. We think we deserve punishment when we fail.
13. We can't take correction or criticism.

14. We rebel against rules, authority, and directions.
15. We go to extremes to gain approval from others.

GRIEVE FOR YOUR LOSSES

If you had a dysfunctional father, your anger is appropriate. You lost the greatest treasure a child can receive—a loving relationship with your father. You carry heavy problems around today because of your dad. An evil has happened, and it was done to you.

Grief is God's healthy process of rearranging the heart to compensate for a loss. It is a safety valve that goes *shhhhhhhhhh* when the pressure from pain builds up too much. If you had a dysfunctional father, your childhood was robbed: You were cheated, and you have suffered a great loss. Grief is essential in the healing process.

Short-Term Gain—Long-Term Pain

These behavior patterns probably saved my life, but they eventually began to destroy my life. As a result, I have been through a long process of identifying and correcting all these patterns, and the function of confession has been essential in the process.

A child does not respond to a dysfunctional father in a godly, mature, intelligent, ethical, healthy manner. The child reacts in whatever way that will contribute to immediate survival, even if it has long-range destructive potential. These desperate reactions solidify and develop into permanent behavioral patterns.

Later in life, these behavioral patterns can turn out to be selfish, harmful, unpleasant, immoral, and even illegal—or, in other words, sinful. Granted: the child established them in a crisis for protection and was ignorant of spiritual morality at the time. But, sin is sin, and sin does damage and needs to be dealt with.

Grief Is a Tool

Grief is not "unchristian." Jesus grieved (Matt. 26:38). The Holy Spirit can be grieved (Eph. 4:30). God grieved (Gen. 6:6). Grief, in its proper use, has God's endorsement. He intends for us to use it as a tool for recovery. You should not avoid grief in the name of stupid machismo. Real men grieve when necessary.

CONFESS YOUR PARTS OF THE PROBLEM

When Dad mistreated me, I struggled to protect myself any way I could. In so doing, I established behavioral patterns that eventually caused me more trouble than my problems with Dad. My learned responses for protection backfired and became a great source of pain. I learned to lie, deceive, manipulate, blame, and avoid responsibility. I filled up with rage, bitterness, rebelliousness, anger, and resentment. I escaped to a fantasy world of books, TV, music, and daydreaming. I developed a mistrust for people—the more you trust, the more you get hurt. I developed nervous tics, a pronounced stutter, and a speech impediment. I never learned to laugh out loud; the most I could muster was a big grin.

Confession is the tool that God gave us to deal with sin. Confession is a practical tool that starts you on the path of recovery by eliminating caustic sin. It can be compared to several functions:

1. Confession is a location device useful in navigation. It is the process of finding out where you are so you can chart a course for where you want to get to. When you confess, you find out where you really are.
2. Confession is a diagnostic instrument useful for spotting trouble spots. It reveals damaged areas that are not functioning properly and, if left unchecked, will lead to greater problems. When you confess, you find out where you are injured.
3. Confession is a cleansing agent useful in purging toxicants from our system. It expels the poison that has been stored up inside us. When you confess, you find out what has been eating you up inside.

To confess means "to agree with God." It means to look at your life as God sees it. It means to allow truth to prevail, to endorse reality, and to line up with God in regard to what He is doing in your life.

As an adult, you must now take responsibility to correct these sinful reaction patterns that you used for protection. These old mechanisms you learned as a child are the ways of man and are ineffective. You must purge them and replace them with God's technique for processing pain.

This action requires using the Bible to identify these thinking, feeling, and behavior patterns and agreeing with God that they are dishonoring to Him, are destructive to you, and work against forming healthy relationships.

You must face and admit your hatred, bitterness, resentment, and rebelliousness to your father (or mother, if need be) to reach the next step of healing. Confession is the process of purging the poison that has built up in you over the years. It breaks down the barriers to recovery.

First of all, go to God and talk it over with Him. He understands and wants to hear you talk about this problem. Then, find a safe buddy with whom to talk this problem through. Bring it up to your E-Team. Get it out in the open. You must talk to another person about it. Finally, talk to your wife about it.

Remember, confession focuses on your sinful response to sinful actions. Confession neither takes responsibility for nor dwells on others' sins: It concentrates on you and removes the chains that hold you back.

I still occasionally ask God to bring to my mind a particular unpleasant incident with my dad and ask Him to help me identify my wrongful emotions and actions in the incident.

I admit my guilt and claim God's forgiveness, which cleanses my heart. It's as if I still have a lot of poison in my heart, and God brings it to the surface, one bubble at a time, to be popped and evaporated forever. More destructive poison removed! More healing done!

FORGIVE YOUR FATHER

We all have a built-in urge to see justice done. If your dad abused you and cheated you out of your childhood, he deserves to be punished. But the sword of justice is heavy, and as long as we carry this burden, we can't be free to love.

Consider Your Dad's Pain

Dr. Jim Wilder, in a personal conversation, gave me some graphic advice on how to forgive my dad. He gave me this scenario:

> Imagine you and your dad standing at the edge of a cliff and a rifle shot rings out from the woods behind. Your dad takes the hit and falls, mortally wounded. Dying, he collapses on you and slides down your leg. He tips you over and you pitch out headfirst over the cliff.
>
> Now you are in trouble and headed for pain and it is not your fault. You are about to suffer great loss. You should be angry. And it was your dad who did this to you. Does it make sense to be angry at your dad and want to go back and make him pay? No. Your dad was shot. He was mortally wounded and in his death throes, he lashed out and tripped you up. Look what was done to him before he did it to you.

Let God Do the Heavy Work

Dr. Wilder told me to rearrange my courtroom. Instead of setting myself up as judge, prosecutor, jury, jailer, and executioner for my dad, I should simply be a witness and let God be all the rest. I should stand before God and witness—just tell the truth. Tell what happened. Then let God prosecute, find guilty, sentence, and execute.

This little process helps me get things in context. It helps me see Dad in a way that makes it easier to let go of my hatred and desire for retribution. I should not, however, use this process to whitewash my dad's actions and say that he was innocent. Men know when they hurt others and often don't care. He had choices and knew he did wrong. He can't get off on a plea of ignorance or temporary insanity. Men are to be held responsible. This process only helps me to understand Dad and let go. It enables me to turn him over to God, who will handle the whole situation correctly and relieve me of having to make things right.

I can trust God to deal with Dad. And He will. God will find Dad guilty because he is guilty. He will sentence him to death and lead him away to his fate. But God the Just is also God the Lover. He loves Amos and your dad so much that He will come down from the bench, walk out to the cross, and die in place of our fathers. Justice then will be served, punishment paid, and fellowship restored. Let God handle your dad. This act will free you to forgive your dad and establish a loving bond with him.

PUT LOVE INTO ACTION

You are not going to believe this, but I actually traveled around the nation and to Europe, South America, and Africa, speaking on the family and how to saturate it with spiritual love while I hated my dad. Can you believe it?

My heart was like a seething cauldron of bitterness and resentment toward Dad. Whenever I thought of him, my stomach knotted up. Whenever I saw a tender father/son scene in a picture, movie, book, or in person, I teared up. I still can't listen to the song "Cat's in the Cradle," by Harry Chapin, without getting gloomy.

After God showed me the hypocrisy of this contradiction, I finally, grudgingly, made a commitment to go to my dad and not merely restore fellowship but to start loving him by faith. I aimed to practice what I preached. But I didn't know how. No one ever told me how to go back and build a love relationship with a dad you hated. I had no clue as to how to heal the damage—to drain the pain pool.

For the Love of Amos

I went home and began loving him by faith with spiritual love. It was hard because approaching home was like entering a vortex of swirling emotional gales and psychological gusts. It was as if a time warp permanently existed near the presence of Major Amos, and every time I drew near, it flung me back to my childhood. Going home felt like reentering puberty. I reverted to the same state of immaturity and anxiety with which I grew up. There was something corrosive in the presence of Amos that dissolved all of my learned adult compensations and coping mechanisms.

The problem with loving Amos is that I had to go back emotionally to my childhood and work through the tangled trauma of trying to love him from a time when I feared and hated him the most. I did not have the luxury of working from an adult vantage point and coping with Dad as an ordinary mortal and peer. As a grown man in my thirties, I still felt paranoid, afraid, inadequate, inferior, stifled, and suffocated in Dad's presence. I always felt guilty and about to be called in to be punished.

This task of loving Dad was the most formidable mission I ever faced because of the troubles in me, not Dad. He had radically mellowed. He became an amiable, folksy fellow always ready with a good yarn. Objectively, I knew he had changed; he was not at all the same man. Subjectively, he overwhelmed me as always. I had to lay a careful strategy and execute my plan coldheartedly and ignore all the frenetic emotions careening around inside me.

I chose a philosophy, developed a strategy, and laid out a sequence of short-range measurable goals that could quickly be accomplished with victory. I knew I had to crystallize my love for Dad and shatter his shell to reach into his heart. I had to x-ray his personality and body to focus on the essence of Amos. I began to see Dad as an eternal soul created in the image of God. Dad underwent immeasurable pain and difficulty through his childhood and life. He was a lonely, isolated man, living with unbearable pain because of the scars and trauma he sustained in his own abusive, tortuous family as a child.

I found him to be a man just like me—lonely, frustrated, and fearful. I trained myself to accept him, love him, and express my affection to him. I ignored, by force of will, his negative habits and made up my mind to demonstrate love to him no matter what I received in return.

I decided that nothing he said or did would swerve me from my path of "love is action" toward him. When he became angry or drunk and started giving everyone trouble, I ignored it and kept on beaming love toward him. When he started needling me to leave the ministry and get a "real job," I just smiled. When he criticized me or put me down, I went out and washed his car or shined his shoes. I actually told him I loved him.

For the Love of Golf

It took time. He became suspicious. He just knew I was setting him up for something. I suppose that no one in the world, besides Mom, had ever acted out love toward him without wanting something in return.

That's when we took up golf together. Dad hated golf. He hated it when he spewed golf balls in all directions, and he never could adjust to the idea of grown men walking around because of these little white balls. Boy, did he hate sand traps and water hazards! He was also a walking beer hazard. He loved beer, and he liked to cuss. He discovered that golf produced a perfect environment for drinking and swearing. He drank about a six-pack every nine holes and careened around the golf course like a runaway stagecoach.

He had a swing like a gorilla and often missed the ball. He had a natural hook *and* a natural slice at the same time. He liked to approach the ball and say, "Watch me hit this one. I'm gonna kill it!"

Bad shots called for bad language. He released great streams of creative profanity that wafted softly across serene greens. He braided together creative and original strands of thundering cuss words in original combinations like the long chains of a complex protein molecule. He had a world-class mouth.

His automatic ritual was to tee up, hack at the ball, cut loose with a chain of blue streakers, take a swig of Falstaff, and then peer out under the bill of his Boston Red Sox cap to see how I would react. So, it was swing, swear, and swig for about 120 shots. (He never counted penalty strokes: "I'm not on the ____ PGA, am I?") And all the time, he watched me out of the corner of his eye.

He was testing me. He wanted to see how his "preacher boy"

responded. He tried to find out how thin my love was for him. Did it evaporate in the heat of bad behavior? Was my love for him thick enough to take it?

About three years before he died, my dad and I finally learned how to express love to each other. We had long conversations together. When I drove home, he would come out of the house, walk over, open the car door, pull me out, and give me a big hug that lifted me off the ground. He had never touched me in all my life except in anger. When I left, he actually told me he loved me.

The tragedy is that we both waited too long before we expressed our love to each other. We only had three good years before he died; yet I am thankful for those last three years. They filled some painful vacuums in my life and helped me feel better about myself. Our restored love did miracles for me, and many of my open emotional wounds healed. Father-love has no substitute.

The above process can work even if your dad is MIA or dead. You need only go to God and work through the court system. I worked through a lot of the above while visiting Dad's gravesite.

Most of you, however, need to go to your dad personally to work through this process. You need to confess your anger to him and purge your heart. Remember, you go to deal with your heart, not expecting your dad to admit or confess anything. Remember, father power does not work upstream. You need to do your part and let him be responsible for his own life.

I'll tell you this: When you go to your dad in the Spirit of Christ, confess your anger, and tell him you want to love him, respect him, and be buddies the rest of your life, it will have an impact on him. He knows how he let you down. He knows about his fatherhood failures. He knows. And he hates it. So when you, the victim, come before him bearing love and goodwill, he may surprise you. Nothing convicts like a victim. This act on your part could be the incident God will use to bring your dad into fellowship with Him.

E-TEAM HUDDLE GUIDE
CHAPTER TWO: Dad the Family Peacemaker

E-TEAM REVIEW
10–15 minutes

After coffee and fellowship, allow each dad to tell about the results of last week's project. This is the accountability part. Be firm with one another and encourage everyone to complete his project. If anyone encountered difficulty or had a family problem arise, pause to allow the E-Team to address the problem and pray.

E-TEAM DISCUSSION
50–60 minutes

This part allows you to discuss the key concepts in this chapter and relate them to your individual lives. Be sure to leave time to complete the workout and encouragement sections.

THE PRINCIPLES (Check the text for help.)
1. Dr. Charles Sell says, "I began to connect the problem with my dad to the problem with my sons." Why do men who did not have good love relationships with their fathers have difficulty with love relationships with their children?
2. What is the Father/Pain/Enmity Cycle? What keeps men from realizing when they have been trapped in it?
3. Why do men have difficulty getting in touch with and facing their pain?

THE IMPLICATIONS (Why are these ideas significant?)
4. What will be the long-range results of a man who does not make peace with his father and who does not deal with the pain in his life? How will his wife and children be affected?
5. Do you know a man who acts gruff and tough on the outside to cover up the pain and hurt on the inside? How obvious is his problem? How do other men respond to him?

THE APPLICATION (How do these ideas affect me?)
6. On a scale of 1 to 10 (1 = extremely bad, 10 = extremely good), tell the E-Team where your relationship with your dad was when you

left home and where it is now.

7. Explain how your relationship with your dad has affected your relationship with your children.

8. What steps in the peacemaking process have you already taken with your dad? Which ones do you still need to take?

E-TEAM WORKOUT
10–15 minutes

Allow each dad to choose one of the project options (plays) to perform during the week. If desired, design your own project. Note: It is essential that each dad make a definite commitment to a specific project before he leaves.

1st PLAY:
  Contact your father and talk about these things. Write a letter, call, or go see him in person.

2nd PLAY:
  Make an appointment with one of the men in the E-Team to get together (try breakfast or lunch) and talk seriously about your relationship with your father. Help each other develop a plan for improvement.

3rd PLAY:
  Make an appointment with your wife and discuss your relationship with your dad and her relationship with her dad. Discuss how both of your relationships with your fathers is affecting your children. Decide on a plan for improvement.

E-TEAM ENCOURAGEMENT
5–10 minutes

Close the meeting in prayer for one another and your families. Include in your prayer a specific request for spiritual power to complete your project successfully.

BREAK THE HUDDLE, GO HOME AND RUN THE PLAY!

The Fatherhood Function: To Bond

Chapter Three
Dad the Family Coach

"I have begun to realize that secure, mature people are best described in nineteen words. They know who they are, they like who they are, and they are who they are. They are real."
— *Chuck Swindoll*

THE BLUE GOOSE

We will never forget the saga of the Blue Goose. We decided to beat the system and take a week-long family ski trip for less than $500. We thought we could do it if we borrowed a motor home and fixed all our own meals: no motel or dining-out costs.

Fortunately, a friend of a friend lent us a motor home, "the Blue Goose." Unfortunately, it was ten years old and needed much repair. Fortunately, we had time enough to get it into the shop. Unfortunately, it wasn't ready until the morning of the day we left. (During the night, every drop of water in the whole plumbing system froze — we didn't know about it until we drove off.) Fortunately, we rushed home, packed up, and got away on time. Unfortunately, we didn't find out about all the problems until we found ourselves in Oklahoma skittering along I-70 with a one-inch sheet of ice, hurricane-type winds, and a blinding snowstorm. Here is what we discovered:

1. The vehicle heater did not work.
2. The propane system on the motor home was broken, and the heater and gas range did not work.
3. The air vents below the dashboard were rusted open and could not be shut. We had jet streams of frigid Canadian air whistling down the Great Plains, into our motor home, and across our feet, legs, and back in the living area.
4. The air-conditioning controls were broken, and the air-conditioning was stuck at *on* at the highest level.
5. The entire water system was out: no sink and no toilet.

6. We were getting about six miles to the gallon.

So there we were, inching across the frozen plains—the family huddled under blankets and sleeping bags in the back, and I totally encased in a sleeping bag with my ski suit on and with my teeth chattering, making more noise than the ice-encrusted windshield wipers. Think of it: Our air conditioner on and vents open in a blizzard.

We finally arrived at the Monarch Ski Lodge, parked in their snowbound parking lot, and started to enjoy our week of no heat and no hot food. We came in off the ski slopes at 4 P.M., trudged to our motor home, ate frozen peanut butter and jelly sandwiches, and crawled into bed at around 6 P.M. because it was too cold to do anything else. We all crammed into one bed and stacked four sleeping bags on top of us. That's the only way we could stay warm through the night.

When we woke up in the morning, Snuffy's (our little puppy) water dish and our pee pot were frozen. The pee pot was a two-liter plastic Mellow Yellow soft drink bottle I had cut in half so Brandon and I wouldn't have to go outside in the parking lot in the middle of the night (the poor girls had to trek to the lodge). At the end of the week, Brandon and I had a cute little stack of yellow-ice hemispheres behind the motor home.

Wednesday night, around 2 A.M., we had a pack of wolves visit the parking lot. When they started howling, we heard the other two motor homes in the parking lot crank up and roar off to town. After the wolves circled our motor home, in the midst of the growling and scratching, I shuffled up to the driver's seat in my sleeping bag and turned the key in the ignition with frozen fingers to discover that the battery was totally dead. We were stranded. After some thoughtful sniffing of the little yellow hemispheres, the wolves finally slinked away, and we were left alone and wide-eyed for the rest of the night.

The whole trip was so ludicrous that it was beyond anger and disappointment. We actually started laughing and joking about everything by Friday. (Hysterical red-eyed gibbering laughter!) As we look back, that trip taught everyone in our family a great many lessons. We learned patience, perseverance, bravery, and how to thank God in all situations.

Adversity bonded us to the Blue Goose, albeit adversity mistaken for fun. Unfortunately, not all adversity falls under the recreation department. True adversity strikes frequently enough. Death darkens every den. Financial ruin, illness, and job loss ruins many families.

Bonding is a choice. Almost anything can be used to bring you closer together. Don't be like the wild mustangs, who form a tight circle and start kicking when wolves attack. They forget to face inward, however; they stand there facing outward kicking the heck out of each other. Face inward and kick outward.

Be like Agent 007 and Bond, James Bond.

NO PEAS IN MY POD

Helen came from Mars, and Brandon shuttled in from Pluto. No way they could have originated on the same planet. They look like humans but, as you would expect, Martians and Plutonians differ radically.

Helen is an excellent cook, but she has never read a recipe in her life. Every batch of cookies she ever made is original; they are like something I have never seen on the face of the earth (Martian cookies!). She takes whatever comes her way. Then she pours, dips, and dumps as the mood grabs her, and waits in palpitating expectation to see what wonders result. People fight over her delicious stuff.

Brandon is not quite so freewheeling. Before building a cabinet for his stereo, he withdraws into hiding and meticulously contemplates the nature of cabinets, calibrates the dimensions of his stereo to the nearest millimeters, ponders design and structural principles, draws blueprints, and engineers his project to its predictable finished precision end.

Shopping is an amusement to Helen. She enters a store, beelines to the third rack on the left section, picks up a blouse (or a sweater or a pair of slacks if that's where she finds herself), marches to the register, pays for it, and moves on to other adventures.

Brandon agonizes over his purchases. He inventories his wardrobe and plots future needs and acquisitions. He studies trends and styles and consults experts. How many seventeen-year-olds do you know have their private subscription to *Consumer Reports?* Then he researches retailers. Finally, after much thought and detailed surveys with friends and neighbors, he makes a careful purchase.

Helen loves to let everyone know all that's going on in her life, and she eagerly shares her colorful emotions. She sometimes calls home from college a couple of times a day. Brandon, like Spock (related to Plutonians?), divulges nothing. His motto: He who has ears, let him wait. He shares about as animatedly as a snail on an iceberg. We call him at college.

KNOW YOUR SNOWFLAKES

Are your kids like mine, or are they from the same planet? Do they seem to be classified in the same phylum? How can the same father and mother produce kids so different?

Kids are like snowflakes. A drop of divine essence forms on your family pane and crystallizes into a unique geometric array of angles, points, slabs, and sheets that mirror a constellation of glittering patterns that stand alone in the universe.

Because they are so different, be careful not to compare your children with others. They are supposed to be unique. Comparison does horrible damage. There are many better ways to tell a child what you respect and expect.

You cannot treat all kids alike. What motivates one, discourages another. What disciplines one, provokes another. What comforts one, enrages another. This makes it imperative that a family shepherd know each child intimately. Knowing your child is one of the primary factors that strong fathers share in common.

A family shepherd must know each child individually and discern his or her uniqueness if he expects to maximize his effectiveness as a family shepherd. His vast arsenal of fathering techniques need to be specially adapted to fit each child individually.

By knowing your child, you not only equip yourself to tailor-make your child-raising techniques to fit exactly, but you also help the child gain self-awareness. A child is born without any knowledge of self. He or she will construct his or her entire mosaic of self-image from the impressions that are reflected by you and your wife. If you don't help your child gain understanding and acceptance of his or her self-identity, he or she will struggle with self for the rest of his or her life.

Chuck Swindoll says it this way: "I have begun to realize that secure, mature people are best described in nineteen words. They know who they are, they like who they are, and they are who they are. They are real" (Swindoll, Chuck, "Your Baby Has Bents." *Discipleship Journal* 47:26, 1988).

It helps to realize how God synthesizes the individuality of a person in order to know your child. Each child unfolds unique crystalline petals of individuality as the result of four separate converging lines of force:

Force #1: The Genetic Endowment.
Force #2: The Divine "Bent."
Force #3: The Spiritual Gifts.
Force #4: Early Environmental Influence (Family).

The parents create Force #4, the early environmental atmosphere that scores so heavily on a child. The dad's role and the impact on families are covered in chapter 5, Dad the Family Pathfinder. The rest of this book also deals with the process of how a family environment marks a child. Meanwhile, this section outlines how God works His will into the fabric of the unique design of a child through the other three forces.

God plays a significant role in the development of the uniqueness of each child because He has in mind a certain destination or role for each person to play in life. This section intends to explain the process and reason for individuality in each of your children; and in light of the destiny of each child, this section underscores the importance of your discerning these variances and nurturing them by your parenting process.

FORCE #1: THE GENETIC ENDOWMENT

Your child has a unique genetic endowment. Some of the child's most prominent behavioral tendencies and characteristics have crouched in hiding for several generations before appearing in your child's genetic code and surprising everyone. Just imagine the rich variety of genetic signals that flow into your child. A child has two parents, four grandparents, eight great-grandparents and sixteen great-great-grandparents. In only one "fourth-generation span," sixteen unique people donate to a child's genetic code.

All Genes Are Not Blue Denim

Recent research of the DNA double helix and "gene mapping" continues to uncover more and more personality traits coded in the genetic material. There has always been a tension among the experts as to what the ratio is of early environmental influences to genetic endowment on the outcome of the child.

Psalm 139, however, speaks without tension while it tells us about the presence of God at the point of conception. As you read this passage, notice two things: (1) the verbs that describe God's handiwork at the point of conception and (2) the number of personal pronouns that confirm the origin of a personal individual soul at the point of conception.

> For Thou didst form my inward parts; Thou didst weave me in my mother's womb. I will give thanks to Thee, for I am fearfully and wonderfully made; wonderful are Thy works, and my soul knows it very well. My frame was not hidden from Thee, when I was made in secret, and skillfully wrought in the depths of the earth. Thine eyes have seen my unformed substance; and in Thy book they were all written, the days that were ordained for me, when as yet there was not one of them (Ps. 139:13-16).

Life Starts with a Winner

When the egg and sperm (the "unformed substance") merge together, two things happen: first, a new human soul begins life; and second, God assigns a specific life span of a definite number of days to the new person. (Make a mental note about "ordained days." I will come back to this later.) Then, in the womb, God begins His unique art form — designer child formation. Notice that the unborn child's soul is not only present at conception, but also be aware of God's artistic engineering.

The Bible uses words like form, weave, made, and skillfully wrought to describe the process that God uses to keypunch His chosen physiological and personality tendencies into the genetic code ("hidden frame") of each child. There is no such thing as a "chance child." Every child is a "designer child." The Scriptures teach that God handles the microscopic substance of each child at the point of conception and starts shaping it according to His will.

It's not a question of which chromosomes are dominant: God is dominant. It's not a question of chance arrangement of genetic material in the double helix: God decides the arrangements. He slices, splices, and stitches genetic material to design the child of His will.

I know that a father releases over 300 million sperm on any given occasion on a snarling chase to be the first to penetrate the mother's egg. I also know about the astronomical computations involved in the possible arrangements of the genetic code imprinted on the DNA molecule. But I know that God, who created all life to begin with, is not perplexed at the task of linking the designated sperm with the chosen egg and shepherding the movements of all atomic parts to predetermined positions to bring forth a child whose name was written in the Book of Life before the foundation of the world, and who has a specific number of days to live. God is God. He can do it.

Who could imagine some sort of accidental child of Aquarius smuggled like illegal contraband through the womb of a woman and delivered to humanity with God blinking in surprise through the delivery-room curtains? Do you really believe you could get a child that God did not preordain for you to have? No, my friend. God understands you and your wife perfectly and dispensed the child perfectly suited to your eternal best interests. Or, He withholds conception for some unknown motive that we can't understand but must accept, by faith, will be in our best long-range interests.

The genetic code represents a major force in the development of your child. Here, God uses a printout on protoplasm, a tangible portion of matter in time/space, as a shaping force, but He also includes a measure of metaphysical input outside the biological process, called the "Divine Bent" to sculpture your child.

FORCE #2: THE DIVINE "BENT"

At last! Medical researchers have pinpointed the location of the human soul in the body. It's in your thyroid gland! Wait! It oozes through the lymphatic system. Maybe it reclines in the liver. I know! It palpitates in the left ventricle. Maybe it tingles through the nervous system? Would you believe the hypothalamus? No, sorry. Medicine doesn't know (although Scripture informs us that life is in the blood—Lev. 17:11, 14). But even if we can't locate it with medical instruments, we can know where it comes from.

Fashions of the Heart

God, in a somewhat mystical way at the point of conception, fashions a "heart" (or "soul"), the essence of a human, and somehow deposits it somewhere in the protoplasm:

> The Lord looks from heaven; He sees all the sons of men; from His dwelling-place He looks out on all the inhabitants of the earth, *He who fashions the hearts of them all,* He who understands all their works (Ps. 33:13-15, italics added).

This passage tells us about the origin of the intangible essence of a human being. The Bible uses words like heart, soul, mind, and spirit to refer to the seat of an individual—the me or the "I-ness" of a person.

This ethereal personhood supersedes the three-dimensional, time/space, physical body. When the body, merely the earthly container or "earth suit," shuts down operations, this innermost essence of a person slips out of the body and enters into an eternal mode of existence. God fashions the heart, pops it into a protoplasmic body at conception, and extracts it when the ordained number of days draw to a close. There are no chance children; there are no accidental deaths.

(Hold on to the phrase, "He who understands all their works." I will refer to this later.)

Flavors of the Heart

God "flavors" each heart when He fashions a "heart" and mixes a "bent" into it. Proverbs 22:6 tells us about this "bent": "Train up a child in the way he *is bent* (should go), even when he is old he will not depart from it."

First, grab the phrase, "even when he is old he will not depart from it." We will soon get back to it.

God assigns "bent" to the heart right after He finishes sorting and stitching the genetic code He desires. No one can know how He does it or how it works. Perhaps it's as if He gently unrolls and superimposes an invisible scroll of time-release personality instructions over the DNA control center. Later in life, this input shows up in special personality traits and preferences.

This insight brings us to a signficant point: There are two contrasting perspectives that describe child-raising—should you function as a sculptor or a gardener? A sculptor sees a vision of the final figure in a block of stone and starts to hammer away, breaking, splintering, and cracking away the pieces that don't belong to his or her vision. A gardener takes the plant and creates the perfect environment for it so it can grow to its full potential. Which concept is best for child-raising?

I believe you are Dad the family green thumb. In Proverbs 22:6, the term "train" means to stimulate a child to self-nourishment, to make a baby want to suck by applying crushed berries to the palate. The phrase "way he is bent" means in accordance with his inner self. The picture I draw from this illustration is one of a father doing whatever it takes to create the required conditions that allow a child to grow naturally to maturity and be true to himself or herself.

This verse does not mean that you should knead, pound, and roll your child like dough; then cut him or her out with the cookie cutter of your choice. You don't fire, bake, and eat kids. This verse does not teach behavior modification. You are not an architect and certainly not a sculptor to cut chunks of your child away until he suits you.

This verse means that we must carefully observe the child to discern his God-given "bent," his unique set of gifts, talents, and abilities, and seek to help the child cultivate and mature them. We need to find the "bent" of a child and encourage the child in that direction. We need to create an environment of acceptance and encouragement, where his "bent" can unfurl and blossom.

For instance, if your child displays a high interest in music, you should encourage music lessons and opportunities to attend recitals: Don't make life wretched for a son by kicking him out onto the football field. If your child shows great prowess in athletics, then encourage it and attend 1 million Little League games: Don't scorch his or her enthusiasm with violin lessons. If your child likes to tinker and take things apart, lock him or her into a trunk to protect your appliances and cars (just kidding). Encourage his or her interests, and the child will grow up to decorate his or her den with patent certificates.

The Dark Side of the "Bent"
Every child should arrive with the label: Caution: The contents of this product may be hazardous to your health. Included in the innermost part of a child are the vestiges of the sin of Adam that has been passed down through the blood of the human race. Every child is born with a sin nature. This "bent" is toxic of a terminal kind: It brings with it damage and death. (Read Rom. 1–9, especially 3:23 and 6:23. Also read Ps. 51:5.)

Every child has sin, but even in sin, each child will have a particular "bent." We all manifest sin in different clusters or combinations of behavior. We all share common *sin* but display different *sins* in our lives. We each have a propensity to express our sin in our own way.

Again, you are not a sculptor—you can never whack sin out of a child. Christ's work on the cross is the only provision for sin. The only hope for your child is to be fused with Christ in His death, burial, and resurrection. But you can and should help a child control the expressions of sin. You must teach the children respect for authority and how to obey—two assets that they are not born with.

The techniques for discipline and training are covered in Volume 3, *Dad the Family Mentor,* but for now, consider yourself a gardener who can reinforce positive growth and discourage negative trends. You can keep poison and weeds out of the way. You may even do a little pruning. But sin is a heart problem, and external motivation, power, and force work only until the teen years, at best. Your task is to stimulate internal motivation in children until they are mature enough to turn the reins over to Christ.

As hired hands, our task must be to channel our children along the path that helps them maximize their potential for God. We don't have to rely on our wisdom to figure out what we want to make our child into. We don't have to worry about creating and patching them into something like a small Frankenstein.

All we need to do is discern the bent of a child and help that child maximize his potential. My job is to create the environment Helen needs to become a world-class Helen. I'm to help Brandon become the world's greatest Brandon. My task is to father my children to get them ready to walk with excellence and victory in the works that God has prepared for them before the foundation of the earth.

I began this section with a contrast of the "bents" of Helen and Brandon. Surprise! They aren't really from Mars and Pluto! They are from Sandy and me, and God put a spin on each that bent them toward certain predisposed inclinations.

FORCE #3: THE SPIRITUAL GIFTS

While the genetic code and divine bent occur at the time of biological conception, the remaining force line from God that converges on your child to make him or her unique comes at the point of spiritual conception. When your child trusts Jesus Christ as Savior, a spiritual birth occurs, called the second birth (see John 3:1-7). At this time of spiritual conception, the Holy Spirit actually enters the body of the child and seals the child for eternal life with Christ.

Now we have received, not the spirit of the world, but the Spirit who is from God, that we might know the things freely given to us by God (1 Cor. 2:12).

Now He who establishes us with you in Christ and anointed us is God, who also sealed us and gave us the Spirit in our hearts as a pledge (2 Cor. 1:21-22).

The Holy Spirit brings incredible advantages to the life of a person. Among His many functions, the Holy Spirit provides spiritual gifts for each person:

Now concerning spiritual gifts, brethren, I do not want you to be unaware. . . . But to each one is given the manifestation of the Spirit for the common good. . . . But one and the same Spirit works all these things [spiritual gifts], distributing to each one individually just as He wills (1 Cor. 12:1, 7, 11).

These gifts differ from person to person: "And since we have gifts that differ according to the grace given to us" (Rom. 12:6).

So we again see the handiwork of God busy designing each person to be a unique one-of-a-kind person. Why? Fix the phrase "for the common good" in your mind and read on to the next section.

DESIGNED FOR DESTINY

It's important to realize that God determines a lot of the distinctiveness of every child. It helps you accept the child, believe in the child, and have hope. God is the One at work here, not some accidental biological protoplasm mindlessly forging random DNA chains. There is no such thing as a chance child. Every child is a designer child, an original masterpiece crafted by God Almighty for His purposes and enjoyment.

From the passages in the section before, I asked you to hold onto these phrases:

Psalm 139:16   "the days that were ordained for me"
Psalm 33:15   "He who understands all their works"
Proverbs 22:6   "when he is old he will not depart from it"
1 Corinthians 12:7 "for the common good"

In pondering these phrases, we lightly brush against heavy matters with serious names like predestination and foreknowledge.

These phrases suggest that God "weaves frames," "fashions souls," mixes "bents," and gives "spiritual gifts" with a predetermined purpose in mind. These actions look forward to specific uses. God has a future mission in mind for each individual child. God gives designer children for designer projects. Each design has a specific destiny.

God established works for us before the foundation of the earth that we should walk in them. Before He pitched the earth in orbit around the sun, God foresaw purposeful human lives brimming with meaningful deeds for Him that would bear eternal fruit and rewards. Working backward from each envisioned life of profitable spiritual labor, He wove frames, fashioned hearts, mixed bents, and provided spiritual gifts to equip each person to fulfill a special destiny.

God has prepared certain works in the future for your child to walk in and a unique slot in the "body of Christ" that no one in the world can fill except your child. You have a designer child for a designer destiny.

The implications for fatherhood are enormous. The true spirit of fatherhood is not to hack out a child the way you want him or her to be. Rather, you are to father with a sense of destiny: You have been assigned to raise a child that God has designed for an appointment with destiny. Your task is to create an atmosphere that helps the child fully develop what God has planted in him or her. You are to help your child become what God wants him or her to be, to do what God wants him or her to do.

You are Dad the Family Coach, with the job of helping your player perfect his or her talent and become all-pro on the Lord's team. Fathering is so much more significant than helping babies grow up. You are involved in the mystical process of helping an eternal soul reach an engagement with destiny.

BONDING BY OBSERVATION

The major theme of this chapter has been knowing your child, which is the key to bonding. There are four ways to increase your knowledge of a child:

1. Direct observation
2. Discussion with your wife
3. Assessment instruments
4. General study

Direct Observation

Why not start a file on each child and become a professional researcher majoring in your child? Through the years, you can accumulate a vast amount of material to put into your child-bonding dossier. You may want to start a *Dad the Family Shepherd Child Biography Kit,* which will allow you to collect and store all the information on your child into one tidy source.

Discussion with Your Wife

A committed father openly discusses his child's development with his wife. He is able to work cooperatively with his wife to find solutions for problems involving his child. He listens carefully and supports his wife in her role as a mother, and he is receptive to the support she offers.

Your wife represents the one greatest source of information you will ever get on your child. She has uncanny abilities to perceive the heart of your child. She has a built-in doctorate degree in the study of your child. Her motherly instinct causes her to scrutinize your child in ways you would never imagine. Trust me: Your wife knows your child.

I recommend setting up a weekly appointment with your resident child expert and gleaning new data on your child from her. Update your files with current information. Get reports from her on behavior, feelings, thoughts, and anything else. Let her have free rein in the discussion, and you will get massive intelligence that will put you way ahead as a Father-Who-Bonds.

Assessment Instruments

Many excellent assessment tools are available to help you gain insight into the nature and uniqueness of your child. Consult your school and church. Write to Dad the Family Shepherd office if you are interested in an excellent professional temperament assessment instrument for children four to fourteen years old. We handle the Performax DISC Child's Profile that measures twenty-four character qualities. It is a twenty-four page, self-grading product for less than $20.00 that reflects the child's opinions of himself or herself.

General Study

When I became a father, there were almost no quality Christian books on child behavior available, but now there are whole sections in bookstores dedicated to the family and the child. There are dozens of excellent books on fathering. You have no excuse, men; the material is out there. Go get it.

To help you get started, I have developed the Child Watcher's Guide (see below).

CHILD WATCHER'S GUIDE
The Ten Phases of Childhood Development

Title	Ages	Description	Crisis
1. The Unborn Phase	−9 mos. to 0	Age of Genesis	Must overcome abortion
2. The Creeper Phase	0 to 12 mos.	Age of Dependency	Must overcome rejection
3. The Toddler Phase	12 to 24 mos.	Age of Exploration	Must establish confidence
4. The Dynamo Phase	24 to 36 mos.	Age of Terror	Must establish ego strength
5. The Social Phase	3 to 5 yrs.	Age of Determinism	Must establish communication
6. The Buddy Phase	6 to 8 yrs.	Age of Friends	Must establish relationships
7. The Modeler Phase	9 to 11 yrs.	Age of Socialization	Must establish social skills
8. The Puberty Phase	12 to 14 yrs.	Age of Transformation	Must establish security
9. The Adolescent Phase	15 to 17 yrs.	Age of Transition	Must establish independence
10. The Quest Phase	18 to 24 yrs.	Age of Dreams	Must establish interdependence

GLAD TO BE ON BOARD

When Helen left for her senior year and Brandon reported to the Razorback football team this fall, Sandy and I entered the netherworld of empty nesthood. We, therefore, rejoiced when Helen and Brandon came home from college a few days ago. In the midst of a hectic football weekend (Arkansas played Ole Miss in Little Rock), we managed to schedule a private family meeting. It was great to have the family gathered together again.

Each family member gave a report on how things were going spiritually, emotionally, and socially. Helen reported on the girls she had in her discipleship group; Brandon told about the Bible study on the football team; Sandy shared about the women's ministry (she's in charge of the women's ministry at Fellowship Bible Church); and I updated them on the state of Dad the Family Shepherd and the Ranch. Then we just sat and talked and sort of loved each other.

As we closed in prayer, Helen and Brandon both thanked God for allowing our family to belong to each other and for the unusual unity and love we feel. They thanked God for allowing them to be on the same college campus together. When we finished, I looked at Sandy, and her eyes were glistening with tears like mine as we felt the incredible bond in our family. I know of no other feeling more pleasurable to my spirit than that of feeling like I belong to a special team. I love the feeling.

This is not an isolated occurrence: Helen and Brandon have both spoken and prayed about family unity from the very beginning. Helen constantly asks me, "Dad, why is our family so close? Why did God bless us with such unity?"

I hesitated to write the above because it might sound too sticky and self-lifting, but I know we have something special. When people ask Sandy and me how our family unity came about, I confess that we didn't do it by design; we were unaware of the process as we went through it. Not until the children were grown, and I started researching family unity and bonding did I begin to understand the principles that built our family bonds.

E-TEAM HUDDLE GUIDE
CHAPTER THREE: Dad the Family Coach

E-TEAM REVIEW
10–15 minutes

Dad, the Family Shepherd
E-TEAM

After coffee and fellowship, allow each dad to tell about the results of last week's project. This is the accountability part. Be firm with one another and encourage everyone to complete his project. If anyone encountered difficulty or had a family problem arise, pause to allow the E-Team to address the problem and pray.

E-TEAM DISCUSSION
50–60 minutes

This part allows you to discuss the key concepts in this chapter and relate them to your individual lives. Be sure to leave time to complete the workout and encouragement sections.

THE PRINCIPLES (Check the text for help.)
1. Explain the three major forces that shape a child that are covered in this chapter.
2. Which one best describes a father's task: sculptor or gardener? Why?
3. What are the four ways Dave suggests to get to know your child better?

THE IMPLICATIONS (Why are these ideas significant?)
4. "There is no such thing as a chance child: Every child is a designer child." What are the implications of this statement on fatherhood?
5. Most American fathers do not know their children well. What reasons would the fathers give for this failure? What reasons would their children give for this failure?

THE APPLICATION (How do these ideas affect me?)
6. Imagine that the E-Team is examining your oldest child for adoption. Give the E-Team a report on why they should adopt your child.
7. Explain the major differences between your first and second child.

E-TEAM WORKOUT
10–15 minutes

Allow each dad to choose one of the project options (plays) to perform during the week. If desired, design your own project. Note: It is essential that each dad make a definite commitment to a specific project before he leaves.

1st PLAY:
Make an appointment with your wife and ask her to answer questions six and seven on page 78 for each of your children.

2nd PLAY:
After talking with your child, make a list of ten things that are important to him. Then schedule an outing with the child to discuss these items.

3rd PLAY:
Start a dossier on each child. Make a list of all the things that need to be in it, including all the information you wish to include.

E-TEAM ENCOURAGEMENT
5–10 minutes

Close the meeting in prayer for one another and your families. Include in your prayer a specific request for spiritual power to complete your project successfully.

BREAK THE HUDDLE, GO HOME AND RUN THE PLAY!

Chapter Four
Dad the Family Catalyst

"Two are better than one because they have a good return for their labor. For if either of them falls, the one will lift up his companion. But woe to the one who falls when there is not another to lift him up."

—Solomon

KILLER CAMILLE

In August 1969, the wench Camille bashed inland from the Gulf of Mexico and mutilated King's Arrow Ranch. The hurricane broke all records for ferociousness. Her malevolent eye passed directly overhead at about 2 A.M., giving Sandy, Helen (two years old), and me a brief respite before resuming her blistering winds of 150 MPH. As we huddled under a pile of mattresses in our little mobile home, the roof finally jostled loose, lifted slowly, and with a roar, snapped away.

The radio gave eyewitness reports of numerous deaths on the coast thirty-seven miles away. It sounded as if the entire ocean had decided to bed down in Mississippi. We had tried to get to the Ranch House several times, but the wind blew the door off and whipped me back across the room. Uprooted trees lay plastered crossways across the windward wall, which sheer wind force held up.

One hurricane can violently spew 60 million tons of water out of the sea. A hurricane can generate more power every ten seconds than the total electrical energy consumption of the United States for an entire year (Paul Tan, *Encyclopedia of 7,700 Illustrations* [Rockville, Md.: Assurance Publishing, 1985], 1357, Illustration No. 6056). This mutant of nature now sought to snuff out our lives.

We sincerely thought we would die. Sandy and I held Helen between us, prayed for a while, said good-bye to each other, and with the calm that comes right before death, we waited for the end. I had made Helen put on some jeans because I didn't want a farmer

80

to find her hanging in a tree the next morning in nothing but a slip.

We were astonished when we awoke at daybreak to find ourselves alive. Nevertheless, the Ranch House was destroyed. Horses were dead and missing. Over 300 trees were down. The air smelled of ozone, wet loamy earth, pine sap, and raw shattered wood.

Our troubles, however, were only beginning. I had just shredded the rotator cuff in my left shoulder while hitting a fullback in a scrimmage with the Pittsburgh Steelers. I was placed on injured waivers and had arrived home a week before. Two days after the hurricane, I got around to opening the mail and discovered that the Ranch insurance had been canceled three days before the hurricane.

I had put the money from my years of pro football into King's Arrow Ranch. We had no financial cushion and no job in pro football. The Ranch was destroyed with no way for it to earn money. No insurance. With an estimate for $50,000 for the Ranch to get back in shape to operate. We had no electricity for six weeks, which meant that there was nothing cold to drink and nothing hot to eat. (I will never eat another Vienna sausage.) We had to get to the highway by horseback for a while until they cleared the roads.

On top of it all, Sandy and I were suffering our worst years of marriage. One could say we were not happy campers.

One year later, however, the Ranch had been completely rebuilt, our camp was full, and our marriage much better. After the whole world had seemed to crash in on us, something happened on the way to despair. We had to make a decision. We had a choice to get divorced, quit the ministry, and walk out of the Ranch and let it rot. Or we could circle the wagons and fight back. We decided to go for the latter, and we made it.

Tragedy happens, but recovery is a choice. We all get sprayed with adversity, but we can choose to let it dissolve us or bond us. We can do either. The choice is ours.

The choice for bonding is always ours. This chapter discusses eight ways to bond your family.

BONDING BY ADVERSITY

The hurricane forced Sandy and me to face our problems. One of the most serious problems was that Sandy had achieved a much higher level of Christian maturity than I. Either I was spiritually retarded or had spiritual crib death. She could outperform me in every Christian activity. Spiritually, there was nothing I could beat her in. She could sing, pray, witness, study, memorize Scripture, and fellowship circles around me.

After a few years of being second best, I, Dad the family competitor, took my marbles and left the game. I decided not to try to be the spiritual leader. The hurricane changed all that. For the first time in her life, Sandy hit a wall she couldn't climb. She was whipped, and her faith left her. She wanted to give up.

A week after the hurricane, my college roommate, John Battle, passed through and made a philosophical statement. "Dave," he said, "God promised that He would stand in front of you and protect you and not let anything through to hurt you. Oh, but, if something gets by Him and hits you — it's not an accident. He let it through on purpose for some reason." Then John drove westward to California. Thanks, John.

Dr. Howard Hendricks, the "Prof" from Dallas Theological Seminary, chartered a private plane and flew to the Ranch. As he surveyed the damage and took stock of the situation, he said, "Well, Dave, one thing's for sure. If God wants you out of this, He gave you a clear signal. But if you stay and recover, you will know it's His will because only He could ever pull this mess out." Then Dr. Hendricks flew westward to Texas. Thanks, Prof.

Gradually, the comments of these wise men sank in, and my faith started to grow. God helped me believe He wanted the Ranch to exist and would use it in a mighty way. Thus, for the first time in our marriage, my faith pulled the family wagon, and Sandy had to hitch a ride.

I received my first taste of having to depend entirely on the Lord. The Christian life actually had been a breeze as a linebacker in the NFL; I trusted God for everything because I already had it all. The breeze became ugly and whipped into a gale force, knocking me out of my self-reliance. I had to trust God in a real way. Many areas in my life straightened out. Some took years. Some, I still struggle with. But I was off and running in the Christian faith.

I broke the cycle of competing, losing, and withdrawing from Sandy. Our marriage blossomed, and she could actually stand me. A few years later, she fell into "like" with me. Now, she's crazy mad in love with me, and I couldn't get rid of her if I wanted to. It all started with the storm. It's an ill wind that blows no good. Camille was no lady, but she blew my marriage around and put me safely to port.

Bonding is a choice. When adversity strikes, choose to let it bond, not bust.

BONDING BY COMMUNICATION

Communication is to the family what blood is to the body. If you desire to bond, you must aspire to talk. The family that talks together bonds together. Strong fathers communicate with their children.

Remember when you dated your wife? Did you think about her a lot when you were apart? Did you like being apart? Remember how you schemed to spend every possible moment with her. You hung out at her house (dorm, sorority house, apartment). You stayed on the phone with her, all night if possible. Remember how you couldn't talk with her enough?

Then you were married, and she assumed you had your tongue surgically removed in a detonguing joint sometime during the honeymoon. You quickly developed the skills of transferring ideas with grunts, clicks, and snorts. You learned the mysterious masculine secret of autopilot speak: the skill of projecting your mind anywhere in the world while your mouth speaks to your wife.

In response, she rapidly mastered a series of sharp one-syllable commands, like: Go! Come! Food! Eat! Fetch! Stop!

This kind of communication is not the stuff from which bonds are built. If you want to bond, you must talk. In *U.S. News and World Report*, Dr. Robert Taylor reports that failure to communicate leads the list of marriage threats:

> The number one reason (for divorce) is inability to talk honestly with each other, bare their souls and treat each other as their friend. . . . I find that too many people talk right through each other rather than to each other — especially when it comes to anything important. . . . Couples who are able to reach a high level of intimacy and interaction tend to stay together. They are the ones who have achieved a sense of shared destiny, of working for a purpose greater than themselves ("Behind the Surge in Broken Marriages," Jan. 22, 1979).

Another attorney has said:

> Couples are divorcing because of their inability to talk honestly with each other, bare their souls and treat each other as their best friend. In my practice, which spans almost 28 years in divorce law, I see people who played games with one another when they were dating in that they

83

always put their best foot forward. They talked about mostly superficial things in order to impress one another.

But after the wedding was over, those couples found it hard to talk, to lay out a week's plan—let alone a life's plan. They failed to anticipate that they were going to change with age and that their interests and ideas would change.

Fathers I classify as deteriorating, inadequate, or abusive score low on child communication. Their dominant characteristic with their children is noninvolvement—they relate poorly to their children. One research study, out of Colgate College, reports that the typical father spends thirty-seven seconds a day in meaningful communication with an infant.

BONDING BY ALLOWING EXPRESSION

Perhaps the most overlooked form of father/child communication is the commitment of a father to allow freedom of expression to his children. When it is overlooked, major damage can occur to a child. Meanwhile, strong fathers score high on allowing children to express their thoughts, feelings, and ideas.

Strong fathers encourage openness by asking questions and listening with interest. They respond calmly to their children's expressions even when they are rude, crude, hurtful, wrong, or inappropriate. They allow children to make mistakes without overreacting. They maintain a sense of humor during these stressful times.

This response does not mean fathers should approve or condone misbehavior; they realize the importance of letting the child be real and free to be open. Then they can deal with the issues, problems, and mistakes in a mannerly, orderly way. I am not at all suggesting permissiveness. It's a question of gaining insight first and solving problems thoughtfully when the time is right.

What I am saying is that it's wrong to block a child's attempts at expression in the mistaken belief that no problems will surface. Don't think that if you can keep the child bottled up, you won't have to deal with any problems. Believe me, you can bury the problems, but they won't die; they will fester and come back from the grave like zombies to cause far worse problems later.

By encouraging freedom of expression without showing anger and rejection, strong fathers gain the following advantages:

1. They can avoid the psychological damage that comes from suppressing a child's feelings and emotions.

2. They promote discovery of the child by exposing the child's heart. Both father and child gain insight whenever a child shares his heart.

3. They build trust with the children and make it easier for the child to admit mistakes and confess sins.

4. They foster a climate in which problems can be dealt with with careful thought and prayer.

My dad could not tolerate any show of emotion by his children. When he fussed at us, he lined us up at attention and, like a drill instructor, he tore us up. He started out slow and deliberate and accelerated, slowly working up into a fever pitch. Then he would start remembering previous crimes and add that to the fire. He reached a crescendo with an eruption of shouting, cussing, and, too often, physical abuse.

My accepted role during these tirades was to stand stone still and freeze my face, my heart, and my mind. A leak of any emotion caused serious trouble. If I got angry or belligerent, I was being insubordinate. If I tried to reason, I was being a smart aleck. If I showed fear, pain, or weakness, I was being a sissy. I couldn't be a person. I couldn't be real. I was extremely defective and worthless; I didn't deserve to be in the family. I didn't belong.

To survive, I learned to play mind games during his tirades. I would count the number of times he used certain words. It was fun to rearrange his face. Rock-and-roll songs wafted through my mind. I solved math problems, scheduled the next day, reran football plays, and escaped into sexual fantasies. I drifted in and out of reality. There is no end to the tricks you can learn when your mind is about to snap.

How do you think all this affected me? When I get under stress, I freeze. I am never comfortable around authority figures. I struggle with a shame-based self-concept. No matter what, I still feel like I don't belong. I always feel like others are "insiders" who share so much in common and I am an "outsider" standing on the fringe. It's "others" and "me."

Believe me, you don't want to stifle your children. A wise father is committed to all forms of communication with his children to form that solid bond and promote feelings of belongingness.

BONDING BY MUTUAL SUPPORT

A simple rule: Children (people) move toward areas that meet needs and away from areas that don't. They move toward love and away from coldness. They move toward acceptance and away from rejection. A father must create an environment where the needs of the family members are constantly met. Dad the weatherman, sets the temperature, controls the humidity, and garners plenty of sunlight for his greenhouse family. This nurturing pulls the family together.

This means that you must know the physical, mental, social, sexual, and spiritual needs of your children at each level of development. Most dads have no clue as to the shifting needs of their children. In their understanding of their children's needs, typical fathers lag about four years behind their daughters and forge about two years ahead of their sons.

The best way to fight the awesome peer pressure during the teen years is to meet the needs of your children when they are infants. If you meet their needs when they arise, you won't have them melting away after puberty. Meeting their needs requires that you hang around with them. You must support them by getting involved in their little enterprises. You need to be there to lift them up when they need it. Though Ecclesiastes 4:9-12 talks about friends, it can be used to describe the importance of sticking with your children:

> Two are better than one because they have a good return for their labor. For if either of them [child] falls, the one [dad] will lift up his companion [child]. But woe to the one who falls when there is not another [dad] to lift him up. Furthermore, if two [or a family] lie down together they keep warm, but how can one be warm alone? And if one can overpower him who is alone, two can resist him. A cord of three strands [a bonded family] is not quickly torn apart.

The family that hangs out together, goes places together, and supports each other in different activities is not quickly torn apart. Here are some examples of how our family bonded by meeting needs:

1. We didn't miss a Little League game. Brandon went through an entire season without a single hit. He batted .000. But he never played a game without knowing that we were in the stands cheering him on.

2. We didn't miss one of Helen's gymnastic meets.

3. Both children played soccer in Dallas, and we never missed a game. One Saturday in late August, it was 110 degrees, but Sandy and I were running up and down the sidelines for both games rooting for the kids. We nearly died, but the kids felt good.

86

4. For a period of about four years, the kids came into our bedroom at night, and I would make up stories and tell them. I created a race of characters — a cross between Bambi and the Hobbits who lived in an imaginary land of thick forests, cascading silver rivers, and large flowered meadows. All the animals could talk. The two main characters were "teenage" deer/rabbit creatures called Runnymede (boy) and Tanyasie (girl).

I had to think of every story I had ever read, steal the plot, and insert Runnymede and Tanyasie. I carefully wove in a good moral lesson for each story. I often stopped in the middle of the story and asked my children what would be the consequences of certain behavior of the characters. Plus, I never finished the story: I would get Runnymede and Tanyasie in a heap of trouble and leave them dangling until the next night.

5. For two years, I read every night to the family from J.R.R. Tolkien's fantasy novels, *The Hobbit* and the trilogy, *The Lord of the Rings*. These stories gripped my children (as well as Sandy and me) like nothing else. It gave them such a rich literary heritage. They heard about vast movements of both good and evil forces and encountered many wonderful personalities. They will never forget Bilbo Baggins, Frodo, Gandalf, Thorin Oakenshield, the Ranger, the necromancer, and the evil orcs and trolls. (As the children grew, we finally had to buy a king-size bed so all of us could fit during story time.)

6. When Arkansas played Tulsa this year, Brandon acquired three tickets from the Athletic Association for himself (he is a red-shirted freshman) and his parents. We signed for our tickets at the pass gate and discovered that Sandy and I had two on the 50-yard line, and Brandon had one in the end zone. I promptly got back in line and traded in all three tickets for three-in-a-row in the end zone. I told Brandon I would much rather sit with him in the end zone than without him on the 50-yard line.

7. Sandy and I have always knocked ourselves out, helping our children throw first-class parties. We constantly encouraged them to have their friends over to our house. We made sure they had great snacks. We helped the children organize their parties around themes and had special projects and games for them.

They picked it up themselves, organizing teenage parties and activities. Brandon would bring a half dozen of his high school teammates home for lunch on game days, grilling hamburgers and fixing lunch for them. On an important night like his graduation, he brought a handful of boys home to eat dinner at our house.

8. Sandy and I tried to make ourselves available to drive the children and their friends around for social activities when they were too young to drive.

Dr. Howard Hendricks was fond of saying, "Be a servant and the whole world will beat a path to your door." I could adapt his words and say, "Be a servant to your kids and meet their needs, and they will beat a path to your heart."

BONDING BY PROJECTS

The first time Brandon ever helped me wax a car occurred in Grass Valley, California, at the home of Sandy's parents, Harlan and Wilma Willey. Before we started, I squatted down close to seven-year-old Brandon and sternly delivered a sobering scouting report on the difficulty of polishing Mr. Willey's car.

"Brandon," I said, "I don't know if we can make it or not, but we're gonna go for it. I can probably get all of it except the front right fender. The front right fender is a tough job for a tough guy. I'm depending on you to finish it off. Together, we can do it, but you've gotta get psyched up for that fender."

Well, Brandon blitzed the fender. He rubbed and stroked and wiped. He whipped that fender for forty-five minutes and shouted at me 100 times, "LOOK, DAD! WATCH, DAD!"

When we finished, I came to inspect and went berserk. I frothed at the mouth and shouted incoherently. I called out the whole family and all the kinfolk and proudly led them on a tour of the front right fender. For the rest of the vacation, I would walk around to the front right fender, shake my head, and mutter to myself. The whole world knew that a shinier fender existed nowhere on earth. Brandon was the champ. Brandon became a professional front right fender polisher and served faithfully at this noble assignment for many years.

Do you think Brandon felt close to me? Do you think we strengthened our bond just a little more? Why? Because Brandon had a skill that he could contribute to bring success to the team. In fact, he was essential and nonreplaceable. Anytime you let someone feel fulfilled by pitching in with the team, you will increase his or her commitment and enthusiasm.

Brandon currently washes Helen's and Sandy's cars all the time without ever being asked. The first time he came home from college, he immediately washed Sandy's car for her as a surprise. Do you think he worked especially hard on her front right fender?

Every time our family tackled a project, we divided up the tasks and assigned them according to the strengths of each family member. When the children were young and we traveled, Brandon would navigate with the map, Helen was timekeeper and would keep us on schedule, Sandy was the treasurer, and I drove. We all took our jobs seriously and made a big deal out of each member's contribution.

Creating a slot where a teammate can make a significant contribution creates intense feelings of belongingness.

BONDING BY TRADITIONS

Every family needs traditions. Traditions provide rich memories that serve to bond a family together. Sandy and I have always sought creative ways to provide "memory builders" for our family. Here are some suggestions.

Take Photographs

Get a good camera and take millions of pictures. It may be expensive, but you can't put a price on the pleasurable memories the pictures invoke in later years. We keep a portrait of Helen and Brandon when they were six and three right by the dressing mirror in our bedroom. Every day Sandy and I look at the picture and just smile.

One of my greatest regrets is that we didn't have an annual family portrait made on the same day every year of our family life. I would give anything to see twenty-four portraits lining our hallway with the evolution of the Simmons family.

Sandy has organized the thousands of pictures we have and put them into albums. We have albums for different years and for different trips. We have a collage of about twenty photos of Brandon at his senior decathlon framed in a 24″ by 24″ frame. Sandy has a photo board in her office with her favorite pictures of the family on it. On a recent trip to Fayetteville (University of Arkansas), Sandy and I noted that both Helen and Brandon had photo boards of the family hung up in their bedrooms.

Celebrate Holidays in Special Ways

Sandy keeps us honest at Christmas. All the rest of us want to open our presents early, but she won't let us. When we get up Christmas morning, I always have a short family devotion to recognize the incarnation of Jesus into the stream of humanity. Before we open presents, we each take down from the fireplace our "Santa stockings" that Sandy secretly stuffs with all kinds of goodies and personal favorites. Then, we pass out the presents. As the family shepherd, I pick up each present and pass them out in turn. Each person must open the present, go bananas, and settle back down before I pass out another present to the next person.

For Thanksgiving, we used to take an annual trip to visit my parents. Since their deaths, we stay at home but try to invite international students or singles without families to Thanksgiving dinner. This year, we hope to start a new tradition of getting together with Margaret, Gracella, and Douglas, my siblings, for Thanksgiving.

Honor Mealtimes

Sandy is a stickler for getting everyone at the table on time and having the radio, TV, and phones turned off. She makes sure we all eat slowly, with good manners, and without outside interruptions. I take the responsibility of promoting conversation. We each usually give daily reports on our day and share interesting developments and conversations. We try not to use mealtime to solve problems or discuss stressful topics. If the conversation lags, I often ask direct questions like, "What was the funniest thing that happened today?" or, "What lesson did you learn about personal relationships today?"

Another idea is to occasionally dedicate a meal to someone in the family, cook their favorite dishes, and honor them with the table conversation.

BONDING BY SHARED PURPOSE

A family should be like an atom. As electrons hurtle around a nucleus, our family revolves around Jesus Christ. Like the incredible energy that holds the electrons in orbit, we have the invisible adhesiveness of the Holy Spirit, keeping us on a flight path of unity. In John 17:20-21, Christ Himself prayed that our unity would be like the oneness He has with His Father:

> I do not ask in behalf of these alone, but for those also who believe in Me through their word; that they may all be one; even as Thou, Father, are in Me, and I in Thee, that they also may be in Us; that the world may believe that Thou didst send Me.

Only as each member walks in Christ can the family experience the mystical union that binds the Christian body—the bride—to Christ, the Groom. Sandy and I trusted Christ in college before we were married. Helen trusted Him when she was three, and Brandon became a Christian even earlier. Thus, our family has had the advantage of unity in Christ for many years.

The Family Commission

All Christians share one thing in common: We work together to accomplish a significant task. In Matthew 28:19-20, Jesus Christ called His people together and challenged them with what we call the Great Commission:

> Go therefore and make disciples of all the nations, baptizing them in the name of the Father and the Son and the Holy Spirit, teaching them to observe all that I commanded you; and lo, I am with you always, even to the end of the age.

A family works as a team to help fulfill the Great Commission. This common purpose unites people in a special way. Nothing compares with the feeling Christians share when they accomplish a mission related to the Great Commission. This bonding process works wonders in families as well.

A team needs a sense of destiny. It needs a sense of purpose for existence bigger than any of the individuals and powerful enough to draw the members together to generate the synergism necessary to accomplish challenging tasks. The greatest task known to human-kind is the Great Commission—to take the claims of Christ to everyone in the world and down through the ages.

The last half of John 17:21 says that our unity in Christ exists for a definite purpose: "That the world may believe that Thou didst send Me." The family exists as a testimony to the bonding and blessing powers of Jesus Christ.

A family does not exist as an end in itself. It has purposes much greater than itself and its members because it affects destinies. The family is God's smallest battle formation and functions as a weapon in His hand in the spiritual battle with Satan. Families live on a battlefield, not a balcony. It fights from a foxhole.

We have drummed this truth into our children before they were even able to understand it. They came into awareness with a worldview that sees the family as the center of a conflict and the need to circle the wagons, and get our backs together to protect one another, and concentrate our warfare outward. Our family exists to act as a witness to attract others to Christ.

Individually, we accept the biblical teaching that people live in spiritual death in a world of darkness and need to become related to God through Jesus Christ. We believe God allows us to live on earth to share the facts on how Jesus Christ's death makes it possible to know God. This purpose lies at the core of our family's being and unites us in a special way. We constantly encourage one another in the task of helping to fulfill the Great Commission of making Christ known. This purpose bonds us in a special way.

How did our children catch this "vision" for ministry? Well, we simply had a Bible study one time when they were young and read them some verses on evangelism; they took off and haven't stopped yet. Right?

Wrong! A vision of destiny and a heart for evangelism cannot be taught. We could never teach or command the kids to capture the "vision." The only way children can receive it is to absorb it.

All their lives, the children have watched Sandy and me praying for others and speaking to people about Christ. They grew up at King's Arrow Ranch, where they sat in on our Bible studies with college students and listened in our counseling sessions. They saw us talk at campfires and teach "Round Ups" to the campers. Their minds are saturated with pictures of their parents ministering to others in a wide range of methods. They learned that ministry is simply a natural way of life.

Our children grew up thinking "ministry as a team." When we lived in Dallas and the kids started elementary school, they became acquainted with a lot of the neighborhood children and became aware of some of the pain the children endured because of a terrible family life. One family had five children each with a different father, and there were strange men constantly visiting their mom. To reach out and help, Helen and Brandon started inviting all of their little buddies to stop by our house early in the morning on the way to school for muffins and hot chocolate. Sandy would then teach a short lesson from the Bible.

The greatest catalyst for mission bonding in our family occurred at King's Arrow Ranch. Both children grew up in the midst of a thriving ministry to college students, high school students, and campers. When Helen and Brandon were still in elementary school, they started working on the high school work teams. While they were sophomores in high school, they moved up to the college level and became bunkhouse counselors. Helen became the director of the girls' camp as a sophomore in college. Brandon became the program director as a senior in high school. The Ranch was a family project. In the last few years, our whole family held top leadership positions, and it was an incredible bonding experience.

BONDING THROUGH THE GENERATIONS

How well you have bonded backward through the generations affects how you bond forward through the generations. Bonding is an art that is passed down through the generations in an almost invisible manner. Families who do it can't explain it and don't understand the problem. Families who don't do it don't know it and don't understand the answers.

America is the land of flatlanders. We are horizontal, stratified, "Now!"-oriented people. We find it difficult to think vertically in generational directions. The modern tempo and mobility have taken us away from our roots. Perhaps the universal access to timepieces has focused us on "day" segments instead of "season" segments. All this squeezes our vision into tunnel vision where we see "here" and "now" and we lose sight of our grandparents and great-grandparents.

You, as Dad the Family Historian, need to give your children a sense of family antiquity and destiny of the kin. Your children need to pick up on the family tree, the family clan, and the family blood lines.

It helps me to know that the Blairs (my mother's line from Scotland) fought in the Revolutionary War. Other Blairs entered Kentucky through the Cumberland Gap with Daniel Boone, and the Indians captured two Blairs in Greyson County. Many of the Blairs fought with the Kentucky Rifles in the Civil War (the War between the States to us Southerners). My great-great-grandfather, Ed Blair, married a Sanders girl whose brother had a boy who knew chicken—he used an ole Kentucky recipe to fry it up right! My great-grandfather helped start and build the church that still stands today in the Mammoth Cave National Park. Grandpa Blair had a whisky still before Prohibition (and during—shhhh!) that went on to become a famous Kentucky distillery after it was taken away from him.

The Simmons came from England and landed in South Carolina. They slowly migrated west and settled in Mississippi in a little community called Simmonsville. My Simmons forebearers were landed gentlemen with sprawling plantations. My great-grandfather was a deacon in a Baptist church. After they lost everything in the War, they left Mississippi penniless and resettled in Louisiana. Meanwhile, Simmonsville dried up and blew away; no trace is left. My grandfather, Luther, owned the first Ford truck in the parish; he had to build the cab and bed out of planks, and it didn't have a windshield.

Much more of the family legends have been passed down, but too much has been lost forever. Mom and Dad used to tell us stories about the "Olden Days." You've heard them too. About how far they walked to school in the snow. How they didn't have shoes. No electricity. Outhouses. Bean diets. Homemade clothes and soap.

All this gives children what I call "Generation Vision." It helps them withstand the incredible pressure that kids have today for "fad vision," where all they think about is the "in" clothes, shoes, music, and slang. Life doesn't start and end with a football game, a date, or a party. Generation vision can help pull a kid out of the mind-charring contemporary scene and into the vertical generation flow. It helps enforce a sense of family identity, permanence, and significance. It makes the family name mean something. It bonds the family.

Before you can push bonding forward through your descendants, you may have to go back to your dad for another shot at bonding with him. The way your dad bonded with you when you were a child seriously affected your "bonding apparatus." If he did well, you probably picked up on it and copied the myriads of details and secrets of bonding without even knowing it. If your dad did badly, your "bonding apparatus" may have been stunted or choked off. You may have to go back, pick up the pieces with your dad, polish off your bonding with him, and then resume the bonding process with your own family.

In my conferences across the nation, I am meeting hundreds of men who have turned their attention back to their dads in their forties. They missed Dad the first time around. Since they have mellowed and have more time, they have become aware of a serious tug pulling them back to their dads who, now in their sixties, have slowed down and make better targets. America is full of white-haired father/son pairs trying to make up for what they missed back in the '50s.

E-TEAM HUDDLE GUIDE
CHAPTER FOUR: Dad the Family Catalyst

After coffee and fellowship, allow each dad to tell about the results of last week's project. This is the accountability part. Be firm with one another and encourage everyone to complete their project. If anyone encountered difficulty or had a family problem arise, pause to allow the E-Team to address the problem and pray.

E-TEAM DISCUSSION
50–60 minutes

This part allows you to discuss the key concepts in this chapter and relate them to your individual lives. Be sure to leave time to complete the workout and encouragement sections.

THE PRINCIPLES (Check the text for help.)
1. Which of the coaching tips on bonding interested you the most? Why?
2. Which are the most important? Why?

THE IMPLICATIONS (Why are these ideas significant?)
3. Explain the difference in a child who came from a family with good communication and one who did not.
4. How are children affected when they are not allowed to express themselves?
5. Should a father just let bonding experiences happen, or should he take the initiative to make them happen? Explain.

THE APPLICATION (How do these ideas affect me?)
6. Tell the E-Team about one of the best bonding experiences of your childhood.
7. Describe the degree of bonding and togetherness in your family of origin. How do you think you are still affected by this today?
8. Tell the E-Team about the most recent bonding experience in your family.

E-TEAM WORKOUT
10–15 minutes

There is only one project (play) this week: Brainstorm for ten minutes on some things you can do to bond your family together this week. Then have each member of the E-Team select one of the brainstorm ideas and go home and implement it.

E-TEAM ENCOURAGEMENT
5–10 minutes

Close the meeting in prayer for one another and your families. Include in your prayer a specific request for spiritual power to complete your project successfully.

BREAK THE HUDDLE, GO HOME AND RUN THE PLAY!

The Fatherhood
Function: To Lead

Chapter Five
Dad the Family
Pathfinder

*"The voice of parents is the voice of God's, for to
their children, they are heaven's lieutenants."*
— *Shakespeare*

COLORS

Brandon developed his first destructive vice when we lived in the condemned old Civil War mansion at the end of the airport runway in Jackson, Mississippi. While Sandy and I directed the Campus Crusade High School ministry in Jackson, we used the old building as an adventurous gathering place for high schoolers, who enjoyed coming around to watch the commercial jets and the National Guard air transports dive-bomb our TV antenna as they took off and landed. Helen had just turned six, and Brandon was pushing four.

Brandon became a TV molester. He gleefully scribbled on our TV screen with many colors of thick-layered crayon. He did his best work with the giant size six-inch Crayolas when no one else was around to distract him.

Not one to appreciate the color balance and composition of his abstract etchings, I warned him to stop and explained the uncomfortable consequences of his misdirected talent. He continued his work, and I stepped up my warning threats.

The Trial of the Innocent Son

Finally, one Saturday morning, I got up early, walked by the TV, and saw a solid sheet of multicolored Crayolas smeared across it. I jerked Brandon out of bed and led him to the scene of the crime. He stood there rubbing his eyes with his little fists and trying to wake up with his 6'4", 240-lb. father looming over him with a glowering look.

I did not lose my temper. I controlled my anger at this threat to my authority and tried to follow the sequence of child discipline that I had recently studied. I wanted him to confess his misdemeanor voluntarily, say he was sorry, and promise not to do it again. Then, I could apply a light little lick or two, forgive him, and then hug and love him.

So, I craftily asked him, "Brandon, my son, tell Daddy. Did you do anything wrong lately? Is there something you did that you have been warned not to do?"

He just stared at me. He had no clue as to what I was talking about. I nodded my head toward the TV and leered at it suggestively. Brandon took the cue and turned to face the obvious evidence.

"Well?" I asked. "Isn't there something you want to tell me, Son?"

Brandon shook his head negatively and said, "Daddy, I didn't do that."

Incensed at his brazenness, I demanded, "Brandon, Daddy told you that you would get spanked the next time you marked up the TV, but I'm telling you now that I am going to spank you twice: once for the TV, and secondly, and much harder, for lying. I will not have a liar for a son. Now, confess to your dad. Tell me you did it."

Again, he pleaded innocent. Then, I began to drift away from the parenting methods I had been trying to master and reverted to some of the ole "Amos" techniques that seemed so natural to me. I snatched him up and blistered him. It was the hardest spanking he ever received. All the while, I kept telling him that I would not put up with a disobedient son who told lies. I figured to nip this in the bud while he was only three.

After the spanking, I gave him one more chance to confess to me and tell the truth. At last! With his little chest heaving and in between sobs, he told me, "OK, Dad, I did it."

About an hour later, we received a phone call from the mother of the family that had been in our home for dinner the night before. She called to apologize over and over because her little girl had just told her that she had marked all over our TV with crayons.

'OK, you stupid miserable excuse of a dad, eat your heart out! You blew it again. And bad."

How do you think I felt? What do you suppose I did?

I grabbed Brandon and crushed him to my chest, hugging him and smothering him with kisses. I held him for an hour. With tears pouring down my cheeks, I repeatedly apologized and begged forgiveness. Since Brandon has always been an instant forgiver, he immediately forgave me. But I went on and made great restitution with many fabulous promises. That rascal ate more ice cream in the next two weeks than he did during the rest of his whole childhood.

What strikes you most about this incident? Did you notice that Brandon reached a point when he became confused about guilt and innocence and confessed to a crime he did not commit? Why? Because his all-powerful father overshadowed him and rewrote history in his mind. Brandon became what his father saw him to be.

Oh, men, the awesome force of father power. It can even make the innocent feel guilty. There exists no other human power greater than father power. God has entrusted this incredible energy/force to us, and so many men don't even realize they have it, much less know how God intends us to use it.

Dr. Henry Biller, today's foremost authority on father research, has written: "The principle danger to fatherhood today is that fathers do not have the vital sense of father-power that they had in the past. Because of a host of pressures from society, the father has lost the confidence that he is naturally important to his children — that he has the power to affect children, guide them, help them grow. He isn't confident that fatherhood is a basic part of being masculine and the legitimate focus of his life" (*Paternal Deprivation* [Lexington, Mass.: Lexington Books, 1974], 145).

All Roads Lead to Dad

Just because a man has lost confidence in his father power doesn't mean it's not effective. It remains the most powerful exterior sculpting force in the life of a child. It slices, gouges, presses, molds, and shapes kids whether the father believes in it, ignores it, or remains unaware of its force.

Father power, applied directly, compelled Brandon to confess to a crime he didn't commit. Applied indirectly in a child's life over a long period of time, it becomes the prime determinant in the following "Big 10" areas of life.

1. Emotional Stability
2. Achievement
3. Relationships
4. Self-Esteem
5. Self-Discipline
6. Family Values
7. Morality and Ethics
8. Social and Political Perspective
9. Spiritual Life
10. Sexual Development

In the study of the development of these areas in the life of a child, research has shown that all roads lead to dad.

Since the birth of social research, father/child studies have been left in the dust compared to the mountain of attention garnered by the superstars, Madonna and Child. In the years from 1929 to 1956, father/child studies received only 11 major grants while mother/child studies cashed in on 160 major grants. Father/child studies grew with the rise of feminism in the late '50s and '60s because the feminists eagerly sought to demonstrate that the mother's and father's influence on children differed little and could eventually be made to be interchangeable.

The findings of the research into the impact of the father on his children surprised the feminists: The difference in the way fathers and mothers affected their children proved to be incredible. Soon, an explosion of research on the father/child relationship by a "rainbow coalition" of sociologists confirmed that the father, as the dominant male authority figure, carried awesome influence over children. His effectiveness/ineptness and his absence/presence, in fact, determine the potential of the children, given a comparable genetic endowment.

FATHER POWER REQUIRES A GOOD MODEL

These discoveries on the incredible impact a father has on his children, for good or evil, makes it paramount that the dad use his father power wisely and serve as a good model for his children. As I often point out, children do what you do, not what you say.

FATHER POWER AFFECTS
EMOTIONAL STABILITY

Paternally deprived boys show more separation anxiety, less satisfying relationships with people, and a greater negative reaction to strangers. When denied access to a masculine decision-making model, these boys have shown severe emotional disturbance.

Paternally deprived girls manifest abnormal anxiety, and their scores are more extreme in temperament and personality tests. When they do not grow up with a warm, affectionate dad, they tend to be more masculine and reject their femininity. Without a dad who distinguishes and rewards their feminine behavior, they are frustrated in forming their sexual self-image.

When there is severe conflict in a marriage so that the father contradicts and degrades the mother in front of the kids, and makes unrealistic demands on her, the children become more emotionally unstable.

Double messages also cause emotional disturbance. If the dad and the mom disagree on child-raising philosophy or techniques, it causes severe emotional conflict. For instance, if the dad is strict and the mom is lenient or vice versa, the kids perceive a double message coming from their parents.

Studies have shown that schizophrenic patients have a high incidence of inadequate fathering (some studies show as high as 75 percent). Abnormalities are directly proportional to the degree of paternal deprivation.

FATHER POWER AFFECTS ACHIEVEMENT

Intelligence scores for both boys and girls in verbal, arithmetic, perception, motor and manipulative spatial tasks increase with the quality and quantity of father/child interactions. In girls, there seems to be a direct correlation between father intimacy and high math scores.

For boys, elementary school is not user friendly. They are socially and emotionally behind girls to begin with, and when they breeze into the classroom, they smack into a host of female authority figures who stress neatness and order passivity and concentration — all of which seem alien to a little boy's nature. Putting boys in a classroom is similar to putting popcorn on a hot skillet: They will shoot off in all directions.

In effect, the school cranks the boys through a feminization process. Studies have shown that boys have feminine behavior reinforced *six* times more than masculine behavior. Furthermore, boys endure latent sexism in class. Female teachers make far fewer contacts with boys, providing boys with less information to their questions than with girls (*Paternal Deprivation*, p. 145).

This means that if a boy already suffers from paternal deprivation, his security will be threatened even more. Dominated by female teachers and outperformed by his female peers, he soon moves to other areas in which to excel and build self-esteem. His scholastic achievement scores suffer. Therefore, boys with effective family shepherds, who reinforce and motivate them adequately at home, will overcome the extra pressure at school and achieve higher.

Intellectual functioning seems to be stimulated by the father's emphasis on instrumental behavior—his "getting the job done" mind-set, his tendencies to encourage exploration and risk-taking, his making decisions, and his solving problems. The more exposure children have to dad's decision-making behavior, the more leadership they display at school. Especially boys with nurturant fathers seem to become motivated to imitate their dad's instrumental behavior. They see themselves similar to their dads. Father/son closeness is definitely related to achievement.

Tests indicate that boys with passive/absent fathers are less assertive, more compliant, more dependent, and more submissive, and they display more immature hostility. Most underachieving boys are alienated from their dads. They have a built-up hostility to their fathers because they feel their dads have rejected them. They feel like failures, and they perform as they feel. These findings are true for affluent families as well as economically deprived families. However, paternally deprived boys do score well in verbal areas.

FATHER POWER AFFECTS RELATIONSHIPS

Studies have shown that the better the relationship between the father and his children, the more they see themselves as similar to their dad and belonging to the family, and the better they relate socially to their peers. A strong, secure family base serves as a solid launching pad for the children to use to project themselves into their turbulent social scene, and the dad is the cornerstone of this foundation.

Father-absent boys end up with better relationships than boys with nonnurturant/present dads. Since they know they have a handicap, they work harder to compensate; whereas boys with ineffectual dads are lulled to sleep and slide unawares into troubled relationships.

Girls who are frustrated in their relationship with their dads are much more critical and aggressive, resorting to acting out their problems socially.

FATHER POWER AFFECTS SELF-ESTEEM

Healthy self-esteem is a result of a good, warm relationship with a father who sets definite, firm limits and enforces discipline in the family. One study showed that 75 percent of schizophrenic women came from homes that had inadequate fathers, who frequently degraded their wives, fought over decision-making power, and employed manipulative techniques to get their own needs met.

Paternal deprivation during the early years (one–five) has a more disruptive effect on the development of self-esteem than at later ages. It does show up later, however. The self-esteem of a college student is positively related to paternal love and negatively related to paternal rejection.

FATHER POWER AFFECTS SELF-DISCIPLINE

Children with good fathers are able to control their impulses, aggressive outbursts, and delinquent behavior. There is less antisocial behavior, such as crime and theft. They can concentrate better and delay gratification.

Father-deficient boys score lower on measures of internal moral judgment, guilt following transgressions, accepting blame, and moral values. The ability to delay gratification deteriorates as paternal deprivation increases. Consequently, every culture, society, and neighborhood where the fathers are absent/passive demonstrates an alarmingly high rate of theft and personal crimes. Gang behavior also increases directly proportional to a father's absence.

FATHER POWER AFFECTS
THE FAMILY VALUES

Children with good fathers are far more likely to develop a high value for the family and make better parents themselves. They tend to marry earlier, stay married, and have more children.

Women who had poor relationships with their fathers tend to avoid marriage and are more likely to seek a career as an escape from the responsibility of working through intimacy with a man. In one study of 100 female executive presidents, it was learned that they all shared these things in common: They were firstborn; their dads had pushed them; they stored their femininity for the future; none had children; and they waited until they were thirty-five to become sexually intimate.

Many of the feminists who seek the destruction of the family suffer from paternal deprivation. Dr. Carl Wilson cites case studies and examples of the histories of many of the leading militant feminists both here and in Europe. He attributes their hostility and destructive anger to a reaction to the pain they had endured from abusive fathers or husbands who had distorted their masculine roles.

One commonly known result of abusive fathers is that they tend to produce children who are abusive to their children. Nothing makes abusive people like abusive fathers. Likewise, an abusive husband will tend to produce boys who are abusive to women.

FATHER POWER AFFECTS MORALITY AND ETHICS

Myriads of research projects show that fathers are the prime determinant in moral and ethical behavior of their children. In many cases the mother talks more about morals and ethics, but the children do what dad does. The father sets the standards and the values.

The social conformity of children depends on the relationship with their father. Bill Glass, former defensive end for the Cleveland Browns and now a specialist in ministering to prisoners, told me, "I have been working with prisoners for many years and have never found one yet that didn't hate his dad. They all love their moms, no matter what her faults. Even if she is a prostitute, they love her. But these men have bitter, simmering hatred for their fathers, or the image their mom gave them of an unknown dad." Prisoners, not noted for social conformity, are largely the result of paternal deprivation.

Father-absent boys score lower on measures of internal moral judgment and guilt following transgression. They will not accept blame, and they reject moral values. Their common bond is resentment against social authority (an extension of father power), and their common expression is counterculture activity. Lower-class boys tend to rebel against the establishment through crime and vice, while middle-class and affluent children attack the establishment by becoming dupes in left-wing social and political movements, or by escaping into subculture pockets or cults.

Children without fathers tend to be more passive and compliant and less able to resist temptation and peer pressure. Strong peer power often overwhelms them so that they compromise what convictions and values they do have and go along with the pack. This behavior sets them up for gang control and antisocial behavior.

FATHER POWER AFFECTS SOCIAL AND POLITICAL PERSPECTIVE

The family is the building block of a nation. The children a family spawns determine the long-run nature and durability of its nation's culture and government.

As the family goes, so goes the nation—and the father makes a family go. The family shepherd acts as the authority figure in the home and determines the character of family government. His sense of values, code of ethics, and concept of personal freedom will affect each family member. The atmosphere that the family shepherd generates determines each member's self-image as a citizen and the ability of each member to practice self-government. A family shepherd makes good citizens, who elect good representatives, who do well running the state.

A dysfunctional family spews out children who carry distorted concepts of authority and government. Paternally deprived families raise citizens dangerous to representative government. If an abusive man heads a family, the individuals from that family will harbor hostility and rebellion, and they will demonstrate a lack of respect for authority. These attitudes will carry over to government authority. In a passive/absent family, the individuals will not understand authority and will react by either passive or aggressive rebellion, or they will desperately seek powerful dominant authorities to "take care of them from cradle to grave."

FATHER POWER AFFECTS SPIRITUAL LIFE

A child relates emotionally to God the same way he learned to relate emotionally to his father. A father conditions a child to relate to a male dominant authority figure, and when the child becomes a Christian, he takes the emotional patterns he developed in the relationship with his father and transfers them to God, the ultimate male dominant authority figure.

In seminary, I took a class titled Theology Proper, which is the study of the attributes and characteristics of God the Father. At the beginning of the semester, the prof handed out a 100-question survey on how we related to our earthly fathers. We took the test, turned it in, and forgot about it. At the end of the semester, the prof returned the same survey but asked us to fill it out on how we viewed God the Father. A comparison demonstrated that each of us emotionally related to God the same way we related emotionally to our earthly fathers.

Men, you represent God to your children until they are at the age where they can begin to relate to God. The emotional patterns and systems they establish with you, the flesh and blood father they can see and feel, will be the same with their Heavenly Father whom they can't see but relate to by faith.

Students with abusive fathers viewed God as cruel and punitive and related to Him with fear and avoidance. Students with passive/absent fathers saw God as abstract, impersonal, and unapproachable.

No wonder I have always been afraid of God and felt guilty and inadequate. I have struggled to relate emotionally to Him. It has taken over twenty years of being "reparented" by God for me to learn to relate warmly and lovingly to Him, to experience Him as a God of love, grace, forgiveness, and as a Shepherd who has my best interests at heart.

FATHER POWER AFFECTS SEXUAL DEVELOPMENT

The father, in his function of launching his children into society, plays the dominant role in enhancing his son's masculinity and his daughter's femininity. Men usually put much greater overt pressure on their sons to adopt the "proper sex role" while they exert a more indirect influence on their daughters.

In their book, *Child Development,* Sueann Robinson Ambron and Neil J. Salkind say, "In gender role development, the evidence points to fathers as having the more important influence, not only in fostering a male self-concept in boys, but femininity to girls. Mothers do contribute to their daughters' adoption of the feminine role, but have little influence on the masculinity of their sons" (New York, Rinehart and Winston, 1984).

In his book, *Paternal Deprivation* (Lexington, Mass.: Lexington Books, 1974), Dr. Henry Biller confirms this view:

The father is the parent most likely to differentiate his children according to sex. Mothers are usually less concerned with distinctive roles for boys and girls, while fathers tend to be quite concerned about their children growing up to be masculine or feminine.

Fathers more than mothers vary their behavior as a function of the sex of the child, and fathers appear to play an especially significant role in encouraging their daughters' feminine development. The father's acceptance and reinforcement of his daughter's femininity greatly facilitates the development of her self-concept (p. 122).

Comparisons of father-absent and father-present boys suggested that availability of the father is an important factor in the masculine development of young boys. There is evidence that the young father-absent boy is more dependent, less aggressive, and less competent in peer relationships than his father-present counterpart (p. 53).

Recently, at the YMCA swimming pool, I watched a young couple teaching a small infant boy how to swim. They stood apart about five feet, and each took turns launching the boy back and forth. The mother would hold onto the child almost all the way. The father would reach out to receive his son but then would back away and coax him to try for a distance record every time. Fathers push limits and urge boys to take greater risks.

On the other hand, dads treat their girls entirely different. They set tighter limits, won't let girls take risks, and even talk to them in a different tone of voice. Watch a man: He will even hold a baby girl differently.

Mothers spend far more time associating with the child during the basic human functions: They change the diapers, nurse, and burp them. They take a more neutral position on sex differentiation: A mouth is a mouth; a burp is a burp; and a dirty bottom is a dirty bottom. Why treat them differently?

Fathers help boys develop a strong healthy masculinity when the boys perceive them as the one who sets limits, makes decisions, controls disbursements of family capital, and administers discipline. Caution: These functions need to be undergirded with consistent affection and caregiving or the child will probably rebel.

Fathers help girls develop strong healthy femininity with the above actions when combined with personal intimacy and desexualized physical contact. When the daughters receive the esteem-building attention and intimacy with their dad, they learn to feel comfortable with masculinity and will relate well to their male peers, pick a good husband, and be a good mother to a son.

An important factor for dads: You may be masculine at work and demonstrate decision-making abilities, disbursement power, and problem-solving skills, but it won't do your children any good unless they see it in the home. If you go home and vegetate into a couch potato, as far as father power is concerned, you are a passive/absent or paternally deficient father. You must show yourself a man in the presence of your children.

Incidentally, almost no other shepherd function can match gender-role differentiation in importance. The very existence of the family depends on the successful perpetuation of gender roles down through each generation. If just one generation fails to raise children secure in their gender-role identity, the institution of the family as we know it could be endangered.

Recent research seems to suggest that the development of gender-role differentiation requires a process of five sequential stages. Each stage requires the child to answer a specific question and reach a certain goal. Each question must be answered and each goal reached before the child can safely move to the next stage. Even though more research is needed, I find these latest theories helpful.

STAGE ONE

Title: The Paternal Differentiation Stage
Ages: 1–5.
Question: "What am I?"
Goal: Gender-role orientation.

In this stage, a child orients himself or herself with the parent of the same sex. A little boy says, "Hey, look! I'm like Dad." A little girl says, "Wow, I'm like Mommy!" This primary step must be completed so the child can develop the security to progress to the next stage. If a boy doesn't have a father or never sees his dad, he can develop an insecurity and confusion over his orientation.

The father displays much more sexual awareness than the mother and consistently relates very differently toward the two genders. Toward the little girl, he tends to protect more, reduce risks, hold more securely, touch more often, and even speak in a more gentle tone of voice. He displays a preference for frilly feminine clothing for the girl. He usually expresses more affection, which is not surprising because the girl is a little replica of the mother whom he fell in love with and married.

Toward the boy, he acts gruffer, treats rougher, speaks deeper, holds with less care, and encourages far too many risks. He lets the boy get dirtier; he mimics fighting, and plays sports to simulate male combat and the hunt. He tends to push the boy a lot more toward achievement-oriented tasks. He rewards the boy whenever he demonstrates characteristics similar to Dad's.

The mother doesn't make much fuss over the genders. She seems more pragmatic and treats them both much the same, as a job: Feed 'em, burp 'em, change 'em, and rock 'em to sleep.

Because of these tendencies, the family shepherd plays the primary role in gender-role orientation.

STAGE TWO

Title: The Heterosexual Stage
Ages: 6–8.
Question: "What do I want to be?"
Goal: Gender-role preference.

In this stage, the child makes a choice: He or she decides to accept or reject the gender role of his or her own sex. A boy will evaluate his father's rewards and benefits for being a male. If he perceives that his dad is fulfilled in his gender role and receives blessings and value from his mother, then the boy will eagerly choose to be like his dad and have the same adventures. The boy will have second thoughts and get confused if:

1. The father seems unfulfilled as a male.
2. The father is absent or passive, and the boy can't take a good reading.
3. The father is abusive, and clouds the issue of fulfillment.

A girl will evaluate her mom on her gender-role fulfillment. If her mom gets plenty of rewards and benefits from the father, the girl will enthusiastically choose to be like her mom so she can get the same treatment. However, problems will arise and the girl will get confused if:

1. The father does not deal with his wife in an understanding way, and she gets cheated.
2. The father is absent or abusive; the girl does not witness her mom getting cherished.

Notice that in each case the family shepherd is the primary determinant. If he treats his wife right, the boy will choose masculinity because the father will get rewards back from his wife, and the girl will choose femininity because she witnesses the rewards her mother receives.

Another dynamic that occurs at this stage is that a child develops a powerful lifelong attitude about the opposite sex. There are two ways this attitude can be created and reinforced:

1. How a child sees the parent of the opposite sex acting toward the spouse.

If a girl sees her father mistreating her mother, she will always be suspicious of men and hold them in low regard. If a boy sees his mother mistreating his father, he will see women as things to be conquered or avoided.

2. How a child relates to the parent of the opposite sex.

During this stage, a child develops a deep hunger for intense affection from the parent of the opposite sex. The boy needs to enjoy an affectionate personal relationship with his mother, the major feminine figure in his life. If he receives it, he will develop the capacity to relate well to women, pick out a good woman to marry, and do a good job of shepherding a daughter. If he doesn't receive it, he will be confused about women.

If his mom is absent a lot, cold, impersonal, too busy or tired, unresponsive, noncommunicative, or doesn't hold and affectionately touch her son, then the boy will grow up doing poorly with women. He will either avoid women or treat them as if they are the enemy.

The girl needs a warm affectionate father who touches her warmly, holds her, and talks to her a lot. If she receives lots of love and attention from the dominant male authority in her life, she will relate well to men, marry a good man, and treat her son correctly.

If her dad is absent, passive, abusive, distant, cold, uncommunicative, or ignores her, she may develop some serious emotional problems. She may grow to hate men and avoid them. Some women develop such intense hostility toward men that they become promiscuous in an attempt to prove that all men are no good. Here's an interesting finding: Prostitutes, strippers, lesbians, and many extremist women libbers despise men, and their feelings can be traced back to the relationship they had with their fathers during the ages of one to five.

Another syndrome that paternally deprived girls often suffer from is a perpetual search for Daddy's love, attention, and approval in other men throughout life. Some women spend their lives going from man to man, from bed to bed, searching for Daddy. Many women marry and relate to their husbands as a father. These marriages are common and filled with emotional upheaval as the woman relates emotionally to her husband like a little girl to her father. This problem adds incredible pressure to their sex life as the wife must contend with the feelings of incest that go along with viewing her husband as her father.

Notice again that the father is the primary determinant. If he relates to his daughter well, she can move to the next stage. Meanwhile, the mother will relate to her son well if she enjoys fulfillment in her gender role with her husband.

(Notice: The most common marriage combination among the parents of homosexuals and lesbians are the passive/absent dad and dominant mom.)

STAGE THREE

Title: The Modeling Stage
Ages: 9–11 or 12.
Question: "How do I act?"
Goal: Gender-role adoption.

In this stage, the child must learn to act out the gender-role characteristics and relationship skills of the parent of the same sex.

Toward the end of the previous stage, the boy wants masculine rewards from his mother, and the girl wants feminine rewards from her father. As they develop this thirst for deep emotional contact with the parent of the opposite sex, it sort of primes the pump. The boy says, "Wow! This is OK. It's fun to be masculine." The girl says, "Would you believe this? How great it is to be feminine!"

They can't have those needs met by a parent; however, since they are too young to marry, God wisely prescribed that the sexual urges go underground and resurface at puberty when marriage and the proper release for sex is an option. As soon as the boy realizes that he can't have Mom, that she belongs to Dad, he resigns himself to settle for someone as close to Mom as he can get. In that case, he starts acting like Dad so he can attract someone like Mom. The girl goes through the same process as she enters the modeling stage.

Here, the boy withdraws somewhat from Mom and attaches to

Dad. He scrutinizes Dad for detailed clues on how to act like a man. What do men do? How do they act? How do they relate to others? What's acceptable and what's condemned in the masculine world?

The girl goes through the same process with Mom.

You will see kids in this stage begin to move out and relate to their peers of the same sex to practice gender-roles with one another. The boys will go crazy over sports. The girls become really interested in womanly things. Each sex will also begin to choose heroes outside the family, settling down to serious hero worship and even reaching the point of impersonation.

One thing you won't see: You won't see them together unless they are fighting. This stage is where little boys hate little girls (they've got cooties) and little girls despise little boys (they are so crude).

STAGE FOUR

Title: The Preparation Stage
Ages: 12–13 to marriage.
Question: "How am I doing?"
Goal: Gender-role confirmation.

This is the gender-role "practice" stage. Launched by cataclysmic hormonal deluges that accompany puberty, in this stage the child is propelled into the heterosexual world to experiment with gender-role responses to peers of the opposite sex. The "young adults" attempt to iron out their sex-role wrinkles with awkward trial and error methods—all to the accompaniment of a spectrum of emotions that range from acute terminal anguish to roof-busting highs. These are the "mate-training" years, where the youths put the finishing touches on their gender role and polish up for marriage.

Success in this stage depends on the proper alignment of the first three stages. If a boy registers male in all three of the first stages, he will feel confident about his masculinity and complete this stage, being successful in his role as a husband and father. If he registers female in any of the first three stages, he will struggle with confusion and doubt about his masculinity.

For instance, if he has a passive/absent father and a dominant overbearing mother who demeans his father, he may reject his biological orientation and decide that he wants to be powerful like his mom. Then, in the heterosexual stage, where he decides his sexual preference, he may choose to align himself with his mother. As a result, there will be a part of him who secretly wants to be feminine.

Or in the modeling stage where he should copy his father (because of the force of his father power), he may copy his mother and absorb her feminine characteristics because she overpowers his weak father. This maladjustment is common among families where the father either travels a lot and is not home much or is home enough but doesn't make his "presence" felt.

STAGE FIVE

Title: The Marital Stage
Ages: The marriage years.
Question: "Do I enhance my mate's gender role?"
Goal: Gender-role fulfillment.

The ultimate purpose of a gender role is to help a spouse feel fulfillment. Men, God did not create masculinity for you. He designed and anointed you with masculinity to enable you to make your wife feel more fulfilled in her femininity. He designed her femininity to make you feel more like a man. Nothing makes me feel more like a man in the whole world than my sparky little Sandy. The greater the contrast, the greater each will feel gender-role fulfillment.

Did you notice that in each stage, the father plays a primary part in establishing proper gender role? No wonder I say, "All roads lead to Dad." The family shepherd acts as a focal image for the children as they develop their concept of self-image, self-esteem, and gender role. If the father is never home or not an active player in the home, the children will suffer to some degree in their normal development stages. Men, your children need a male authority figure in the home far more than they need you to make a lot of money to provide for them.

THE DEAD-END ROAD: NO OUTLET

As one investigates the impact of early environmental influence (family) on a child, it becomes obvious that the roads to Dad are the most traveled. Dad is dominant. He is the prime cause, the initiator, the head. Every family is a reflection of the father, for good or bad. For the healthy functional development of all ten of the above areas, Dad the family shepherd must have his act together.

E-TEAM HUDDLE GUIDE
CHAPTER FIVE: Dad the Family Pathfinder

E-TEAM REVIEW
10–15 minutes

Dad, the Family Shepherd
E-TEAM

After coffee and fellowship, allow each dad to tell about the results of last week's project. This is the accountability part. Be firm with one another and encourage everyone to complete his project. If anyone encountered difficulty or had a family problem arise, pause to allow the E-Team to address the problem and pray.

E-TEAM DISCUSSION
50–60 minutes

This part allows you to discuss the key concepts in this chapter and relate them to your individual lives. Be sure to leave time to complete the workout and encouragement sections.

THE PRINCIPLES (Check the text for help.)
1. Of these ten areas in which fathers affect their children, which one did you find the most interesting? The most surprising? Explain your answers.
2. What other research information can you share with the E-Team about how fathers affect children?

THE IMPLICATIONS (Why are these ideas significant?)
3. Summarize the positive results when children have a strong, nurturing family shepherd.
4. Summarize the negative results when children suffer paternal deprivation.
5. Currently, over 60 percent of black births and over 30 percent of white births are to unwed mothers. These babies will not have fathers. Thousands of other children have fathers who abandon them. What problems do you predict in the future for our country because of these circumstances? What is being done now to solve these future problems?

THE APPLICATION (How do these ideas affect me?)
6. Tell the E-Team how your dad affected you in one of these ten areas.
7. How are you affecting your children in one of these ten areas?

E-TEAM WORKOUT
10–15 minutes

> Allow each dad to choose one of the project options (plays) to perform during the week. If desired, design your own project. Note: It is essential that each dad make a definite commitment to a specific project before he leaves.

1st PLAY:
   Pick three of these ten areas that you feel you need to improve on the most with your children. Then choose one that you want to start with. List and implement three ideas to help with your first area and begin praying about the other two.

2nd PLAY:
   Make an appointment with your wife and take turns discussing how your fathers affected you in several of these areas. If you mention some negative ways, talk about how you can forgive your father and how you can overcome the negative effects.

3rd PLAY:
   Form a committee of concerned men in your community and discuss what you can do to help children without fathers.

E-TEAM ENCOURAGEMENT
5–10 minutes

> Close the meeting in prayer for one another and your families. Include in your prayer a specific request for spiritual power to complete your project successfully.

BREAK THE HUDDLE, GO HOME AND RUN THE PLAY!

Chapter Six
Dad the Family Manager

"For God, a plan is a statement of fact.
For man, a plan is a statement of faith."
                                    —Pat McMillin

THE BIG WINNER/LOSER

Frank, the miracle worker, had won big again. Another string of victories that day polished off a spectacular week of accomplishment. Sitting in his corner office perched atop a prestigious skyscraper in lower Manhattan, Frank had secured a series of patent registrations in Germany, sold off an unprofitable subsidiary in Ohio, signed a new contract with a Japanese firm, and switched advertising agencies. Not a bad week of work.

He left the friendly cooperative office smiling, caught the commuter, and started toward home. An hour and a few drinks later, he found himself in his Mercedes, driving slowly by his home time after time as he aimlessly circled the block. His euphoria gone, his confidence shattered, he was trying to get up enough courage to enter his home, his failure zone, and face his wife and children.

Frank went through this ritual every day. He would leave his successful career at the office only to enter the family fiasco in the evening. Each day, he trudged from the penthouse to the outhouse. He was a scintillating property in the corporate world of finance and management but a frozen asset in the domestic world of women and children. Frank could do no wrong at work, but he did all wrong at home.

The question is, how could a man demonstrate outstanding leadership in the marketplace, but at home even the dog ignored him? Why can't a good leader at work make a good Dad the family leader? You may not shift between such extremes as Frank, but I bet you have noticed this enigma in your own life: Why is it harder to provide good leadership in your home than just about anywhere else?

My good friend, Dr. Charles Sell, recently presented the following ideas at a convention of fatherhood experts that gives helpful insight into this phenomena. Basically, men are prone to achieve much more at work than at home because of the following reasons:

1. Men are endowed with natural strengths more suited to success at work. Therefore, men are encouraged and rewarded in their efforts at work, and they consider the family as a lower priority, even expendable.
2. The skills and talents that contribute most to success at work often cause the most trouble at home.

Dr. Sell supplied this chart to contrast the difference in the dynamics of work life and home life.

Dynamics at Work	Dynamics at Home
Production	Relationships
Prestige	Love
Power	Negotiate
Things	People
No Feelings	Feelings
Support System	On Your Own
Vast Training	No Training
Supposed to Be Work	Supposed to Be Easy
Quick Product	No Product
Quick Feedback	Slow Feedback
Clear Rules	Vague Rules
Clear Roles	Confusing Roles
Can Replace People	Lifetime Tenure
Can Take Another Job	Lifetime Tenure
The Bottom Line	The Heart

(Dr. Charles Sell, Lecturing notes at Fathering 91 Convention, Lake Geneva, Wisconsin, March 1991)

When a man spends his whole life fine-tuning all his abilities to excel in the work environment, he alienates himself from his home environment. When he spends the entire day immersed in the work mode, it's almost impossible to cross the threshold of his home and switch over to an entirely different operating mode.

No wonder so many men work late and delay reentry. Dr. Sell says, "A workaholic is not one who loves to work; he just doesn't like it when he is not working."

Can a man learn to master this daily leadership switch and be a champion manager of his home? And if so, how?

Of course he can if he uses King David's philosophy of the balanced management approach described in Psalm 78:72: "So he shepherded them according to the integrity of his heart, and guided them with his skillful hands."

King David shepherded his people successfully with a balance between a heart focus and skillful management technique. This chapter takes this philosophy and offers practical coaching tips on how to help you:

1. Focus on improving your heart management.
2. Focus on adapting your management skills.

THE HEART PART

The Tin Man from the Land of Oz would have made a poor father because he had no heart. It took a little girl, Dorothy, from Kansas, to help him get a heart. If you want to win with your children and wife, you must perfect "heart management" techniques.

Have a Heart for Your Wife

The best thing you can do for your children is love their mother, your wife. For decades, family research keeps showing one fundamental law of the family: Parents who love each other produce healthy children. They are filled with love and have plenty left over to pour into their children.

In their excellent book, *Love Is a Choice*, which I highly recommend, Hemfelt, Minirth, and Meier present this concept brilliantly. Each parent has a legitimate need to receive and store love in a "love tank." As they bond together, they establish connecting pipes to fill up each other's "love tank." When they remain in fellowship with God, He pipes His love downward. The love the parents receive from God and each other keeps their "love tanks" brimming and ready to overflow. They are like living springs who never run dry.

At birth, these "full love-tanked" parents bond with the child, connect their pipes, and begin the two-decade process of filling up the child's love tank. A child with a full love tank feels accepted,

significant, and secure. That child will have an excellent chance to:
1. Develop a healthy self-esteem and avoids a severe shame-based core.
2. Develop a trust in his or her parents and believe in the family system.
3. Develop a respect for authority and work through the growth phase of independence to the mature phase of interdependence.

The child grows up healthy, weans away from the family of origin, bonds to a mate, and makes good pipe connections with the next generation.

If the parents do not love each other and/or are cut off from God, however, they do not have a fresh supply of love in their love tanks and their love resource dries up. People without love fill up with pain. Instead of love lakes, they develop pain pools. Pain-pool people throw up defense mechanisms and pain killers, which form barriers that make it even harder to get love piped in. The pipes become clogged, pinched, and sometimes totally shut off.

Love-thirsty parents cannot impart what they do not possess. They become like sponges, not springs, soaking up love wherever they can find it. They frequently try to reverse the natural flow with their children and force the children to pipe love backward into their own dusty love tanks. They become takers instead of givers. Thus begins the process that leads to a classic dysfunctional family.

Children with empty love tanks feel rejected, abandoned, and worthless. They have an excellent chance to:
1. Develop a negative shame-based core and begin to develop defense mechanisms and pain killers. They will suffer damage in their hearts and will have difficulty thinking, feeling, and acting correctly.
2. Develop a mistrust and resentment for their parents and lose faith in the family system.
3. Develop a contempt for authority, reject their parents' standards and values, and struggle for power. It won't take long for them to outgrow and go out—to become too big to control and turn to outsiders to have their needs met.

Children grow up with low "love tanks" and repeat the cycle with their children (the sins of a father are visited on his descendants for as far as four generations). Gary Kiker, a therapist for RAPHA, says:

A child feels like two people — ½ Dad and ½ Mom. When one parent rejects the other parent, the child feels split down the middle and ½ rejected. He loses the ability to relate to the rejected parent.

If the parents reject each other, the child feels totally rejected — his or her love lake disappears and his or her pain pool fills up. That child grows up dysfunctional and passes it on to the generations to come.

Your child is the flesh and blood of your wife. If you love her, you will love the "her" in your child. Also, if you are bonded with your wife, you will feel good about yourself and will like the "you" in your child. Likewise, a daughter feels loved when you love your wife because she knows that so much of your wife is "in her." The same is true with your son when your wife loves and respects you.

Of all the things you can do to bond with your children, loving and bonding with your wife is by far the most strategic and effective. If you do nothing else, bond with your wife, and childbonding will naturally follow. The father/mother bond sets the tone for the home and establishes the standard for bonding.

Just to be aware of the need for a leadership switch as we leave work and enter home is half the battle. We men aren't heartless robots — we simply get locked into our productive mode and cruise into the home on auto pilot. We lose our context and forget to turn the switch. We need to set up some prompters to trigger the switch and jolt our minds into family focus.

I established visual prompters to prepare me for reentry (reenter the presence of my family after I have been away). On my route home, I have designated several visual indicators that remind me of Sandy. Each time I think of one on the way home, it activates thoughts of Sandy, and I begin to discharge the energy of my male work drive and pick up on Sandy and my home. The last "Sandy Prompter" is the antique pot-bellied stove she refinished with her own hands.

When I walk up the steps and see that stove, I remember to complete the switch and wire into my home mode. I walk into the house, track her down, make eye contact, say her name, and start talking to her. This process is not natural with me, and I struggled with this reentry problem for years. Nevertheless, the "heart prompter" system is a coaching technique that has produced great results for me.

Have a Heart for the Lord

Men, we can receive great insight on home management by studying the leadership style of Jesus in His role as the "Groom" of the church:

> For the husband is the head of the wife, as Christ also is the Head of the church, He Himself being the Savior of the body. . . . Husbands, love your wives, just as Christ also loved the church and gave Himself up for her (Eph. 5:23, 25).

The Bible tells us to copy the leadership style of Jesus, which was characterized by love more than anything else. His love motivated Him to give Himself up — to be a Savior. Saviors go to death for the ones they save: That's what saviors do for a living — they die. Jesus demonstrated loving leadership, and He bids us to do the same. This means that we should love our families enough to be willing to do whatever it takes to make sure our family members reach full potential.

Have a Heart in the Right Place

Good leadership is balanced leadership. The mark of a man is to keep his priorities balanced. After years of study and consultation, I have discerned that there are twelve major priorities that a man needs to be concerned about and keep in balance. I have arranged these priorities into three groups:

1. Mission Priorities: Eternal relationships that we are assigned to cultivate.

2. Resource Priorities: Temporal things that are allowed to accomplish our mission priorities.

3. Personal Priorities: Personal gifts that help us accomplish our mission priorities.

In the Dad the Family Shepherd Video Conference, I devote an entire hour to the management of our priorities, but here we have room only for a graph that shows the twelve major priorities in balance.

My major thesis in priority management is this: Priority management is heart management. If your heart is right with God, your priorities will be right.

THE SKILLS PART

Having acknowledged the difficulty in making the switch from workplace leadership to home leadership, let me hasten to say many

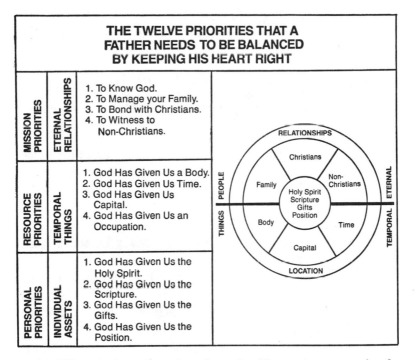

THE TWELVE PRIORITIES THAT A FATHER NEEDS TO BE BALANCED BY KEEPING HIS HEART RIGHT		
MISSION PRIORITIES	ETERNAL RELATIONSHIPS	1. To Know God. 2. To Manage your Family. 3. To Bond with Christians. 4. To Witness to Non-Christians.
RESOURCE PRIORITIES	TEMPORAL THINGS	1. God Has Given Us a Body. 2. God Has Given Us Time. 3. God Has Given Us Capital. 4. God Has Given Us an Occupation.
PERSONAL PRIORITIES	INDIVIDUAL ASSETS	1. God Has Given Us the Holy Spirit. 2. God Has Given Us the Scripture. 3. God Has Given Us the Gifts. 4. God Has Given Us the Position.

work skills can be adapted and used with great success in the home. The skills of planning, problem-solving, resource management, and crisis management that you had to learn to make a living can also help make a family. As a review to some and an introduction to others, I am providing a "Reader's Digest" quick-start management course of work skills for your consideration. I am also providing some case studies to show how they are used in the home.

Dad the Family Planner

In his indomitable way, Professor Howard Hendricks constantly punched home the urgent need for planning in the ministry and the family. With his unique style, he tossed us these management gems in seminary:

If you don't know where you are going, any road will get you there.

If you aim at nothing, you will hit it every time.

The definition of a fanatic is one, who having lost sight of his objectives, redoubles his efforts.

God the Master Planner

Even God plans. He doesn't operate by shooting from the hip. Isaiah 46:10-11 tells us about God the Planner:

> Declaring the end from the beginning and from ancient times things which have not been done, saying "My purpose will be established, and I will accomplish all My good pleasure." . . . Truly I have spoken, truly I will bring it to pass. I have planned it, surely I will do it.

Before the first minute ever clicked off on the clock of time, God determined the end—the way He wanted everything to work out. He planned the world before He ever started it. He assures us that He is in control and we are exactly on schedule. His "purpose" and "good pleasure" are happening the way He planned. We have a definite God with a definite plan. He emphatically insists His plan will absolutely happen. Count on it.

He not only has a plan for the world but also one for each individual. In Jeremiah 29:11, God says, "For I know the plans that I have for you . . . plans for welfare and not for calamity to give you a future and a hope."

Although God is speaking to Israel, the principle applies to the church and to us as individuals. God wants us to have hope.

These two verses should be a great encouragement to family shepherds because they assure us that God is sovereign and that He is in control of a predetermined plan. We each play a role in it, and His part for us is ultimately one with great benefits, not one with calamity. This means that He wants you to have hope for your family *no matter what shape it's in now.* This verse can be applied to your life and family at any point, like, right now!

You don't need to let any previous disasters or problems ruin your family. They may still affect you. If you stick your finger in a fire, it will hurt for a long time. The past, however, doesn't have to control your future. You can't change the past, but you can change the future that past was headed for. Just stop now, claim these verses, and expect God to place you on the path to hope. It's not by magic. It won't happen automatically. You have to give your life to Christ, live by the power of the Holy Spirit, and apply Scripture in your life. This plan is what He has for you to give you hope instead of calamity.

With this in mind, our plans for our families and careers take on a different perspective. We shouldn't be trying to predetermine what trip we want to take and letting God, the great Bellhop in the Sky, carry our luggage. Planning becomes an exercise in discerning God's will for us and conforming our lives to it.

Management consultant Pat McMillin says it this way: "For God, a plan is a statement of fact. For man, a plan is a statement of faith. Planning is predetermining the course of action that will take us from where we are to where God wants us to be" (Class notes from DME 803: Administration for Progress, Reformed Theological Seminary, Jackson, Miss., Summer 1986).

The Reasons for Planning

He who wants to—plans: There is no plan without desire. The extent and quality of your planning is directly proportional to your commitment to it. Therefore, here are eight reasons you should be Dad the family planner:

1. God plans and encourages us to plan (see Prov. 15:22).
2. A plan is a motivational tool. A clear, positive plan that shows great promise of success causes people to be enthusiastic.
3. A plan is a communication tool. It provides a common reference point and clarifies assumptions.
4. A plan sets the context for decisions. No decision is ever made in a vacuum. A plan gives you a benchmark with which to make comparisons and evaluations.
5. A plan gives confidence. It allows you to see that something is possible. If you can see a solution on paper, you can have hope that you can make it a reality.
(Casey Stengel said, "They say you can't do it—but sometimes it doesn't always work." Yogi Berra said, "The fans don't always want to come out to the park, but you can't stop them.")
6. Planning saves time. Planning is the process of allocating time to its most significant use.
7. Planning saves worry. Without a plan, you see glitches waiting in ambush at every turn of the road. A good plan minimizes things that can go wrong. Mark Twain must have been a good planner because he said, "I'm just an old man who has known many troubles but most of them have never happened."
8. Planning tells you what to do next. Consultant Bob Biehl wrote: "After seriously studying leadership for over two decades . . . consulting with more than 50 CEO's and talking to literally hundreds of leaders in all walks of life, I summarize leadership as: Knowing

what to do next, knowing why that is important, and knowing how to bring the appropriate resources to bear on the need at hand" (Lecture notes at Masterplanning Associates Conference, Vail, Colorado, April 1981). A plan helps you know these items.

The Steps of Planning

1. Establish your value system.

You must have a system of values, a code of ethics, a set of priorities, and a list of convictions to serve as parameters in your planning. These things help you by giving you tracks to run on. You won't waste time developing a plan with steps that violate your values. Your value system not only affects your plans, but they also help you select your goals. An example: I want Helen to cope successfully with common problems when she goes off to college.

2. Define your goals.

A goal is a specific, measurable, realistic statement of action that can be scheduled and accomplished. They should be used as targets, not whips. They should be used as carrots, not cattle prods. Begin with prayer. Think of conditions you desire to exist as a result of your efforts. Then, think of an action that, if achieved, will contribute to the condition you desire. When writing a goal, begin with the word *to,* include a verb and noun. Use a quantitative word. Here is an example: *To* have Helen change the oil in her car before she goes off to college next month.

3. Locate the starting point.

Carefully evaluate your starting position by finding out exactly what conditions exist and what resources you have with which to begin. How can you get where you want to if you don't know where you are? Have you ever received directions to a location that started from a point you never heard of? Helen knows how to measure her oil level, but she doesn't know where the oil pan, the plug, or the oil filter are located. She doesn't know what kind of oil and filter to use, and she doesn't know the sequence or how often to change the oil.

4. Develop a strategy.

Brainstorm and list all the tasks that must be done to reach your goal. Consider the budget and organize all resources. Put all tasks in sequence and schedule them. Consider effectiveness (doing the right things) and efficiency (doing things right). Think through the critical path (what absolutely must happen for success). Define your failure points (what might happen to stop us). Set up a tracking process to keep things on target.

Here is my strategy to help Helen learn to change oil:

1. Read the manufacturer's manual by Friday.
2. Send her to the store to buy the filter and oil.
3. Get her a bucket, crescent wrench, an oil filter wrench, and some towels and gas for cleanup.
4. Have her take out the oil plug and drain the oil.
5. Have her twist off the oil filter.
6. Have her put on the new filter and put the plug back in.
7. Have her pour in the oil and check the level.
8. Have her clean up.
9. Go bananas and brag about her in front of everyone.

Case Study: The Plan to Climb the Mountain

Helen and Brandon were about nine and six when we camped out in Colorado on the bank of a little creek gurgling along a forested valley in the Rocky Mountains. Our camp was perched at the base of a rather small hill, which the kids thought was the biggest mountain in the world. They pestered me to death trying to persuade me to take them mountain climbing—the thing next to suicide on my list of fun things to do.

I soon realized I would have no peace until we scaled the hill (mountain). I decided to use this activity as a training project to teach the children about prayer, planning, and perseverance. We held a planning session and established our goal: To use teamwork to climb the mountain in time to see the sunset behind the mountain range west of us.

We prayed: They asked God to help them; I prayed that God would give us a plan and help us stick to it and be successful. I remember asking that each one of us make it to the top *without any help from me.* Sandy prayed for team spirit, relationships, fun, and fellowship. We estimated how far it was and what rate we expected to maintain. We planned breaks, water, and food. We appointed a timekeeper. We tethered the dogs, loaded up, and started off.

Ten minutes later, they wanted to rest though we still had another twenty minutes until our first scheduled break. We got badly off the plan. We became exhausted. We were losing our light. About halfway up, they did what I just knew would happen: "Daddy, please carry me." No way! I refused. I reminded them of the plan and prayer. They claimed further revelation—God didn't insist on reaching the top, just a good effort. It was mutiny on the mounty.

I would not let them quit. We took many extra breaks, but we didn't quit. They whined and cried, and Sandy was getting mad at me for being so resolute. We finally made it up to within fifteen feet of the top when they stopped, refusing to go any farther. We talked it over, and I reminded them of the goal, the plan, and the prayer. After they revived, we went up and over the crest—right into a small herd of deer.

Since the deer could not sense us below the edge of the hill, we shocked them when we popped up. They shot into the air, darted about, and scattered. The kids went nuts with excitement. We scoured their little plateau home and found all kinds of horns, bones, and other deer artifacts. After a while, we settled down to watch the sunset and built a little fire.

The children wanted to commemorate this adventure. We had just studied in the Book of Joshua how the Israelites, when they crossed the Jordan River, put big stones in it to remind them and their descendants about what God had done. Helen and Brandon jumped up and built a pile of stones to commemorate how God had helped them make it to the top. Somewhere, on a little foothill in the Rockies, there is a small pile of stones put there as a testimony to how a good plan and God's assistance helped the Simmons family crest the top.

Dad the Family Problem Solver

Even with a good plan there are many things that can go wrong that require some problem-solving skills. Too often, fathers move right along until they meet a problem that wrecks them. Professor Hendricks says, "The measure of a man is not what he accomplishes but what it takes to stop him" (Class notes from CE 729: Principles of Discipleship, Dallas Theological Seminary, Dallas, Texas, Fall 1979). Many times the problems that stop us could easily be solved if we used a proven process.

I have studied management under many great mentors, such as Professor Hendricks, Bob Biehl, Roc Bottomly, Pat McMillin, and Tom Landry. I have read Peter Drucker and many other famous management gurus. I have compared and contrasted all their systems of problem-solving. From their work, I have synthesized them into a seven-step process.

1. Focus.

Pray and make sure you have clearance and direction from God. Get your bearings — your context. Remind yourself of your purposes, objectives, and other parameters wherein you wish to work.

2. Identify the problem.

The more precisely you define the problem, the better the solution. For best results, write it down and read it aloud.

3. State the objectives.

This step is the most frequently skipped. Failure to state your objective precisely in clear, measurable results makes it impossible to develop a clear path to its solution. It is essential in teamwork because everyone needs to be working together rather than against one another.

4. Brainstorm.

This is the creative part and is usually cut off before completion. People usually think of one idea and run with it. They fail to consider alternatives that allow for debate and choice. The idea is to generate as many ideas as possible without any evaluation during this process.

5. Decide on the plan.

Take the different alternatives and measure them according to your precise statement of objective, making sure it's in your parameters. Choose the best alternative. It will usually be the shortest, simplest, and the one with fewer moving parts. The more things that can go wrong usually will.

6. Act.

Implement it. No solution is worth anything if it never is tried. In the book, *In Search of Excellence*, the author states that the number one characteristic of excellent companies is their ability to act. Digital Equipment has the motto, "Do it, fix it, try it."

7. Evaluate.

Afterward, check out the whole process and look for ways to improve.

Dad the Family Troubleshooter

Every family is faced with a crisis from time to time. Strong fathers know how to handle them. They know the only safe way to handle a crisis is to handle it before it ever happens.

Tom Landry, former coach of the Dallas Cowboys, taught me this lesson. I watched him carefully on the sideline during the game.

When something went wrong, Coach Landry never panicked or had to scramble and guess how to handle the crisis. In fact, he never had to solve a crisis on the sideline during a game. All he had to do was *remember*. He just *remembered* what his plan was in handling a crisis.

Long before the game, Coach Landry imagined everything that could possibly go wrong and developed the best plan to resolve it. He did his crisis management before it became a crisis so he wouldn't have to make decisions under stress and pressure. This way, he entered the game with the best solution for every crisis that could happen.

I applied Coach Landry's principle to my family and developed emergency plans in case we ever had a crisis. When our children were young, we had a plan in case there was a fire in the home or in case we were about to have a car wreck. My children knew what to do if some pervert ever offered them candy. They knew what to do if Sandy or I were ever rendered unconscious. They had a plan to stay out of a fight or win if they couldn't. They knew what to do if they ever became lost or were left alone.

What would your family do if you suddenly died? Do they have a plan to see them through? Howard Dayton, Jr. of Crown Ministries has developed an incredible tool especially for this crisis. In case of your death, it tells your family everything they ever need to know to carry on with a minimum of disruption. Write to Dad the Family Shepherd if you would like information on this product.

Dad the Family Financier

No doubt you know the woman with bouncing checks who claims the problem is not that she keeps overdrawing, but that her husband keeps underdepositing. Do you also know the man who thinks that he has money in the bank as long as he has checks?

The Bible has much to say about money and its role in our lives. Howard Dayton, director of Crown Ministries, reports: "There are approximately 500 verses on prayer, fewer than 500 on faith, but more than 2,350 verses on how to handle money. Moreover, Jesus Christ said more about money than any other subject."

The way we view and use money can make or break us (and our family). It has direct consequences in the way we relate to the Lord. Our relationship with Him goes up or down according to the way we handle money. In Luke 16:11, Jesus says, "If therefore you have not been faithful in the use of unrighteous mammon, who will entrust the true riches to you?"

Money is a test to see what's in your heart. If your heart has a spiritual policy regarding money management, God will trust you with managing other spiritual commodities. If your heart is not right about money, you will fall into serious problems and also disqualify yourself for further use.

How to Get a Money-Ache

Money is the problem that divorcing couples most often verbalize. But they are fooled. It only appears that money has caused their marital discord. The truth is they have had their hearts so jerked out of kilter that their value system has flopped upside-down. Money problems only reflect heart problems.

Since money measures the value of your wealth, it acts as the leading indicator of the true priorities of your heart. What your heart considers valuable will be seen in the way you handle money. Your money will hit whatever target you aim your heart at. You can't see the invisible shots your heart takes, but you can sure find out about it by putting a tracer on your money. In Matthew 6:21, Jesus says, "For where your treasure is, there will your heart be also."

When a family hits a stress streak over money, you can bet they have a serious heart problem. Money is like a stress headache: Whenever your heart starts getting stressed, you get a money-ache.

The Two Banking Systems

My close friend and associate, Dan Dantzler, has helped me more than anyone to understand the significance of money in our lives and the contrast between the two money philosophies that exist in the world.

There are two power blocks in the world competing for the allegiance of human hearts: God's power system and Satan's power system. Each uses a philosophical system about money as a major tool to recruit men and women to their ranks.

Basically, the contrast centers on the perspective of God's involvement in the daily transactions of our lives. The world sees God as absent/passive and money as a measure of wealth. The Bible sees God as total master over all resources and money as a measure of faith. The following is a more detailed description and contrast of the two systems:

The World's Philosophy of Money

It starts with a view of the world as temporal and material—a theory that physical well-being and worldly possessions constitute the highest value and greatest good in life. Each person controls his or her own financial fate, though luck can play an important role. People earn money, own it, and control its use. Since money is the measure of wealth, the goal is to accumulate as much as possible for personal benefits. If there is a God, He doesn't actively participate in the marketplace or in financial matters: He stays in His own safe zone.

The Biblical Philosophy of Money

It starts with a view of the world as eternal, physical, and spiritual—a theory that intangible values from the spiritual world supersede all earthly material concerns. God has ownership and control over *all* spiritual and physical things and allocates them to us to manage for Him and for His purposes. Since money is a measure of faith, the goal is to trust God for all provisions and disbursements. God has total control over the marketplace and all financial matters. God is the safe zone. (See Luke 16:9-13; Matt. 25:14-23; Phil. 4:11-13; Deut. 10:14; Ps. 50:10-12; Matt. 6:19-34; Col. 2:6-9; Heb. 12:1-2; 1 Cor. 4:2; 1 Chron. 29:11-12.)

The Bible doesn't say wealth is evil. It is the love of wealth to the exclusion of seeking godly things that is wrong. A heart can't show concern for God when the materialistic philosophy contaminates it. Therefore, working backward, when you see a person who does not manage money according to scriptural rules, you are looking at a person with a cardiac control problem. The world controls his or her heart, and money is the symptom.

Can you imagine a nurse reading a patient's thermometer, shattering it on the floor, and screaming, "More degrees! I hate those evil degrees. Quick, let's get rid of those degrees, and, sir, would you kindly stop accumulating them?" No, the degrees are like money: They are neutral and serve to tell you what's going on inside.

Body heat is essential, but it can increase too much and cause damage. You don't hate the indicators.

Thousands of healthy families get into serious trouble because they don't understand the incredible contrast between these two opposite and conflicting philosophies about money. From this soil of philosophical ignorance sprout many startling money weeds that intensify all other family problems that happen to be present.

The Bible says deceptive philosophy about the world captures men and women. The worldly philosophy of money sneaks in with such innocence, grabs thousands of Christians, and enslaves them without them ever knowing it. To some, it looks harmless. To most, it doesn't even appear as a spiritual issue. The Bible, however, warns us about these dangers:

> But a natural man does not accept the things of the Spirit of God; for they are foolishness to him, and he cannot understand them, because they are spiritually appraised. But he who is spiritual appraises all things.
> — 1 Corinthians 2:14-15

Many American Christians are deceived and live in a make-believe dichotomized world that looks like this:

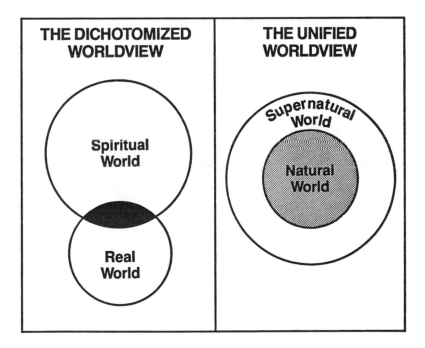

THE DICHOTOMIZED WORLDVIEW

Spiritual World

Real World

THE UNIFIED WORLDVIEW

Supernatural World

Natural World

Though they wouldn't articulate it in this way, they really see it like this: You have the real world (material world), where tangible physical things happen according to visible laws, and you have the spiritual world made of parts of life in which religion plays a role. Christianity concerns itself with things like worship, guilt, family, mental health, relationships, and social betterment. God is over the whole world, but He restricts His operations to the safe zone and isn't really involved in the material world of work, money, and sports—except for the 10-percent cut with which He funds His sphere of influence.

We all know this attitude of Christian materialism exists, yet I have never found an individual who will admit to being guilty of it. It's always "Someone else, not me. I'm mainstream!" Families drift into it and never realize it, and it eats their hearts out.

You, as family shepherd, need to understand how these two systems work and how to stay plugged into the right one. You also need to master the principles of family budgeting and family accounting. Detailed help on money matters lies beyond the scope of this book. Therefore, I recommend the following books, which you may order from Dad the Family Shepherd:

Your Money, Frustration or Freedom, by Howard Dayton (Wheaton, Ill.: Tyndale House, 1979)

Your Finances in Changing Times, by Larry Burkett (Chicago: Moody Press, 1975)

Master Your Money, by Ron Blue (Nashville, Tenn.: Thomas Nelson, Publishers, 1986)

E-TEAM HUDDLE GUIDE
CHAPTER SIX: Dad the Family Manager

E-TEAM REVIEW
10–15 minutes

After coffee and fellowship, allow each dad to tell about the results of last week's project. This is the accountability part. Be firm with one another and encourage everyone to complete his project. If anyone encountered difficulty or had a family problem arise, pause to allow the E-Team to address the problem and pray.

E-TEAM DISCUSSION
50–60 minutes

This part allows you to discuss the key concepts in this chapter and relate them to your individual lives. Be sure to leave time to complete the workout and encouragement sections.

THE PRINCIPLES (Check the text for help.)

1. Discuss ways your work life is different from your home life.
2. Why is loving your wife one of the best things you can do for your children? What do children experience when their parents dislike each other?
3. Explain the difference between the world's philosophy of money and the biblical philosophy of money.

THE IMPLICATIONS (Why are these ideas significant?)

4. Why is it important for children to see their father plan, solve problems, handle a crisis, and allocate resources? How will children be affected when they never get to see their dad do these things?
5. Explain the statement by Pat McMillin: "For God, a plan is a statement of fact: For man, a plan is a statement of faith."
6. Why is money such an accurate measure of a man's value system? How does God use money to show a man where his heart really is?

THE APPLICATION (How do these ideas affect me?)

7. Discuss ways you can improve on the process of transition from work mode to home mode.

8. Tell the E-Team which of the twelve priorities in your life need to be brought back into balance. Which ones are you neglecting? Which ones are you overdoing? What would your wife say about your priorities?
9. Define materialism. Discuss with the E-Team how a man can determine if he is too materialistic. How can you help a man who is but won't admit it?

E-TEAM WORKOUT
10–15 minutes

Allow each dad to choose one of the project options (plays) to perform during the week. If desired, design your own project. Note: It is essential that each dad make a definite commitment to a specific project before he leaves.

1st PLAY:
Make an appointment with your wife and explain to her why it is so difficult to make the transition from work to home. Ask her if she has any ideas on how to make the transition smoother. Ask her what she can do to help.

2nd PLAY:
Make an appointment with your wife and discuss the difference between the world's philosophy of money and the biblical philosophy of money. Discuss materialism and evaluate where your hearts are on this issue. Using the planning steps in this chapter, make a plan to improve in this area.

3rd PLAY:
Brainstorm with the E-Team and come up with some ways you can help your children learn the biblical philosophy of money and commit themselves to it.

E-TEAM ENCOURAGEMENT
5–10 minutes

Close the meeting in prayer for one another and your families. Include in your prayer a specific request for spiritual power to complete your project successfully.

BREAK THE HUDDLE, GO HOME AND RUN THE PLAY!

Chapter Seven
Dad the Family Counselor

"We have renounced the things hidden
because of shame."

—Paul

DESPERATELY SEEKING ERASURE

I first became aware of my need for erasure when I entered the fifth grade back in 1953. It was a big year: Two-tone cars had just hit the market; Dad was reassigned from Ft. Riley, Kansas, to 5th Army Headquarters in Chicago; we moved to Hammond, Indiana; I started my first real job—delivering the *Chicago Tribune;* and our family bought our first little black-and-white TV. I realized I was fit only for erasure.

Yes, it's true—I deserved to be erased, eliminated, purged, eradicated, excreted. My main goal was to vanish. What other conclusion can a young boy make when he is not allowed to want, think, feel, or do anything on his own?

If a father deprives a boy of all the things that validate personhood, how can the boy consider himself a person? He soon perceives that he is a defective mistake that accidentally exists and should be dispensed with.

Television changed our personal lives forever, not because it made us quit family conversation, but because it showed us that we never had any. We had been having monologues, with Dad talking and the rest of us nodding. Dad chose the subjects and formed opinions; our job was to confirm and verify. No one was allowed to disagree with Dad. Dad exercised total control, but we didn't realize it so much until the TV arrived.

It wasn't just that Dad decided what TV programs the family had to watch. He also decreed which programs we had to *like* and which programs we had to *hate!* We had to like Roy Rogers, "Dragnet," and Jackie Gleason, but we had to hate Lucille Ball, Desi Arnaz, and Sid Caesar. I had to love Ted Williams and the Boston Red Sox. I had to hate the New York Yankees. I had to love Bob Cousey and the Boston Celtics.

The sad part was that Dad selected shows, people, and games to watch based on what he disliked the most rather than what he liked. He preferred to watch critically; that is, he enjoyed criticizing more than being entertained. He would rather watch the Yankees play and pull against them than the Red Sox play and pull for them. Of course, we had to follow suit.

There arose in those days a boy driven to rebellion. He grew up, stretched forth his hand in anger toward his father, shook himself free from his kin, and departed to the wilderness to seek his own way. He charged out to make his mark, but he soon discovered that he didn't know what mark to make. He looked within and saw only his father. He searched in vain for the boy that should have been there but, alas, he was not there, for he had been stolen. His anger burned and his heart grew cold as he beheld his loss. And indeed, his loss was great.

DETERMINISTIC FATHERHOOD

Modern research methods confirm the biblical truth about how certain fatherhood styles compel their children to rebellion. H. Stephen Glenn, a noted authority on American youth, reports some startling findings about parenting style and youth reaction in his book, *Raising Self-Reliant Children in a Self-Indulgent World* (Rocklin, Calif.: Prima Publishing and Communications, 1989, 212–14).

He cites a study completed by Dr. Fred Streit, which relates the perception that 6,000 teenagers have of their parents and their involvement with drugs and alcohol. Glenn writes:

> The results were clear and intriguing in that it was possible to explain the use and abuse of the different drugs by looking at how the adolescent perceived the way his or her parents were acting.

Setting up a matrix using an x axis of love/hostility and a y axis of permissiveness/strictness, the researchers designated the following parenting styles on Chart A. Chart B shows the common drug of choice as correlated with the corresponding parenting styles as perceived by the children.

In explanation, Glenn writes:

When young people perceive their parents' control over them as loving, designed to move toward autonomy, and when they believe overall that love, care, and respect dominate, they perceive the relationship with their parents as low risk, stable, and low in stress.

Chart A   **Chart B**

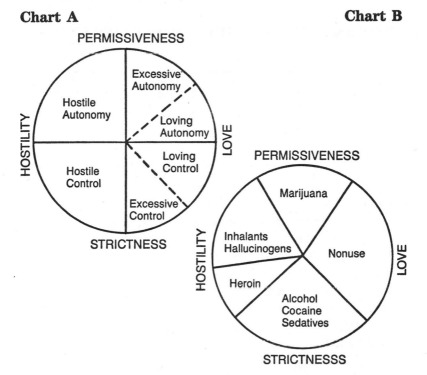

The teens who perceived their parents' behavior *inside* the areas of Loving Autonomy and Loving Control indicated fewer behavioral disorders and nonuse of drugs and alcohol. The teens who perceived their parents' behavior *outside* the areas of Loving Autonomy and Loving Control indicated excessive drug and alcohol use.

This study also shows a relationship between negative behavior and the increase of hostility and strictness. In other words, the more children are exposed to harsh rigid rules without nurturing support, the more they demonstrate rebellion, aggressiveness, antisocial behavior, sexual promiscuity, and lack of sensitivity to others. They will rise up and throw off their parents and their value system.

Management Style Dynamics

The Fourth Generation Rule follows a specific process that can work in a positive fashion that will help develop an honor-based child with inner peace and good relationships or in a negative fashion that will cause a shame-based child with inner turmoil and strained relationships.

The process that leads to an honor-based heart looks like this:

PROCESS CHART FOR THE HONOR-BASED CYCLE

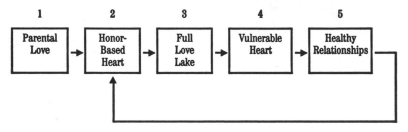

1. Parental Love:
   The child receives nonperformance spiritual love.
2. Honor-Based Heart:
   The child feels "I am worthy."
3. The "Love Lake":
   The child fills up with love and has needs met.
4. A Vulnerable Heart:
   The child becomes transparent and real to others.
5. Healthy Relationships:
   The child develops interdependent relationships.

The end result of this process is the joy that comes from mature, healthy relationships. The child receives spiritual love that builds an honor-based heart with enough security to allow the child to be real and genuine with others. This openness allows genuine intimacy and honesty in relationships in which all parties can practice biblical "body life" principles of mutual encouragement, admonition, and accountability.

However, this process can work in a negative way.

The alternative system to the honor-based system starts with performance-oriented human love, which leads to a shame-based heart and two major problems in a person's life: first, it wrecks his or her ability to relate to others; and second, it leads to addictive behavioral disorders. It was a problem in my family of origin, and it affects around 95 percent of Americans. It follows this process.

PROCESS CHART FOR THE SHAME-BASED CYCLE

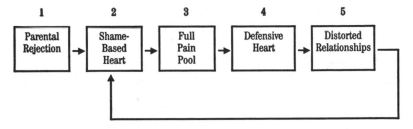

1. Parental Rejection (Lack of Love):
   The child perceives rejection.
2. Shame-Based Heart:
   The child feels "I *am* a mistake."
3. The "Pain Pool":
   The child fails to process pain and stores it.
4. A Defensive Heart:
   The child builds protections to hide his or her heart.
5. Distorted Relationships:
   The child develops dysfunctional relationships.

This chapter deals with the dynamics of the shame-based system and explains God's strategy for switching to an honor-based system. You, Dad the family counselor, need to master these principles in your own life and be able to help your family do the same.

MANAGEMENT BY SHAME

At this time in my life, I have faced the reality of being a shame-based person and have begun the process of healing that requires a basic understanding of how I became that way. From years of research, hours of counseling and therapy, and careful analysis of how being a shame-based person played out in my life, I offer these thoughts on shame-based dynamics. I hope these thoughts will persuade you to contemplate your own life and puzzle through these issues yourself or aid you in understanding and helping those around you.

The Shame-Based Cycle presented above works in this way: A child perceives rejection from the parents and concludes that he or she is defective (shameful). Flooded with the pain that shame causes, the child establishes a system of defense mechanisms and pain killers to protect his or her heart. These behaviors disrupt relationships, which leads to more feelings of rejection. The cycle then continues. Here are the steps of the Shame-Based Cycle that you must understand to be an effective Dad the family counselor.

Step One: Rejection (Lack of Love)

When a dad, the dominant male authority figure, provides an ample supply of love, nurturance, and positive reinforcement, the child develops a healthy positive self-concept. That child thinks, "If my all-powerful father feeds me positive feedback and accepts me, I must be significant and am of great worth. Therefore, I am honorable."

Unfortunately, it doesn't work that way in every home. Too many children feel rejection from their fathers (and/or mothers); and there are a variety of ways that parents make their children feel rejected.

1. Conditional Acceptance

There is something about dads that puts their children under unreasonable performance standards. Even the best fathers induce more shame than they realize. Every child acutely feels the intense pain that comes from disappointing Dad. It is almost impossible for a child to feel like he or she measures up to what Dad wants. When he or she doesn't, more shame enters into the system. Think about your dad and how you feel about the way you satisfied his expectations.

Conditional acceptance leads to two of Robert McGee's false beliefs (he is founder of RAPHA and author of *Search for Significance*):

● I must meet certain standards in order to feel good about myself.
● I must have the approval of certain others to feel good about myself.

A child with these false beliefs entrenched in his or her heart sets himself or herself up for constant rejection and ensuing shame. That child thinks: "I am defective because I am not perfect. I deserve rejection and always will because I will never be good enough."

2. Abandonment

When a child perceives abandonment, shame pierces the heart. Abandonment is passive or covert abuse. It may be harder for the parent to recognize even though it hurts the child just as much as overt aggressive rejection. Anything that generates the feelings of aloneness, neglect, or separateness in a child will create shame. Whenever a child feels he or she can't depend on his or her primary caregiver for nurturance and protection, that child feels abandoned and exposed.

Lack of love, discipline, caring, interest, attention, rules, personal boundaries, time, focus, listening, and talking characterize abandonment. It is pushing the child out too early and too fast. It is neglectful fatherhood. Unfortunately, some current trends in parenting are actually serious forms of shame-inducing abandonment. This list includes:

● In two-career families, latch-key children have no one to come home to after school.
● In two-career families, child-care children spend the preschool years in institutional facilities.
● Parents are absent from athletic functions, dance recitals, school plays, and the other activities.
● Parents excessively use discretionary time without the children, such as sports and travel.

These children think, "If Dad really loved me, he would spend time with me, love me, talk to me, nurture me. He wouldn't be away so much. Since he doesn't do these things, there must be something severely defective about me. I am a mistake. I am a shame."

3. Negative Dominance (Excessive Control)

Negative dominance or excessive control means an obsessive need to control another person to satisfy an unhealthy need. (This statement does not refer to the normal child-raising function of discipline and establishing healthy rules. See Volume 3, *Dad the Family Mentor* for a full explanation on dominant control and personal boundary violation.) This situation is when a parent dominates a child (or spouse) to the point where the child begins to lose identity.

In a way, this bonding or unity is carried to an extreme. Since the lines or boundaries of personhood are violated, individual people become blurred into a soupy morass instead of a matched set of unique individuals. The diagram shows a healthy togetherness where each person maintains a distinctive self. The diagram on the right illustrates negative dominance: One person has consumed the other. (When two amoebas merge it's not called bonding; it's called feeding.)

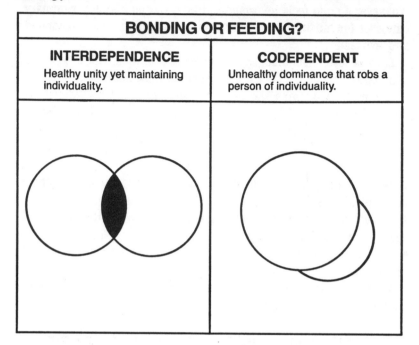

BONDING OR FEEDING?	
INTERDEPENDENCE Healthy unity yet maintaining individuality.	**CODEPENDENT** Unhealthy dominance that robs a person of individuality.

The child is denied the normal personhood functions of thinking, feeling, and choosing. This is what happened to me in my family of origin. I had to abide by the party line and follow politically correct thinking, feeling, and choosing. We had a big list of emotions that were never to be expressed. Furthermore, there were certain problems and conflicts that could not be mentioned — much less worked through.

I became an extension of Dad: He made me into a clone. The word that clicks with me is "erasure." I was a person worthy to be deleted. I was the incredible shrinking son. Shame on me for wanting to be a person!

Don't be fooled! A negative dominant father comes in more flavors than a drill sergeant. No greater power exists than an alcoholic or chemically addicted father as he mobilizes and manipulates his family into an elaborate protective and rescue system. He gets them to invest their whole lives into sustaining him. As the family completely loses its identity, it exists only to enable him to continue his addiction. An addictive person holds the whole family hostage. Their identities are submerged, and they become dysfunctional.

Laboring under excessive control, a child victim believes, "I do not matter. I am unimportant and expendable in the care and feeding of others. I might as well not exist. I feel pushed out and not worthy to belong. I feel rejected and full of shame."

4. Hostility

Hostility, rage, and anger lash out and whip the self-esteem of a person. When a child lives with a caustic, negative, critical authority figure, that child blames himself or herself for the hostility of the parent, internalizes guilt, and builds a shame base.

The child who suffers under hostility thinks, "Surely, authority figures are correct in their appraisal, and if I am the subject of such displeasure, the fault lies entirely with me. I deserve rejection. I am defective, not the authority. I deserve the blame. I am a shame."

The first step in the shame-based cycle, rejection, can be caused by a variety of ways and brings the child to the next step, developing a shame-based heart.

Step Two: Shame-Based Heart

God created us to share His honor-based nature with Him. He made us for fellowship with Himself and intended to take delight and pleasure in knowing us. It all started with Adam, Eve, Cain, Abel, and Seth—the first dysfunctional family. The original sin of Adam and Eve brought about separation from God, and this rejection caused them to develop a deep base of shame.

They passed their sin and shame traits down through all of their descendants (Rom. 5:12). Therefore, we all start life with a sinful nature and a shame-based identity, and we cannot measure up to God's standards (3:23). We are not what we were meant to be because we feel the deep shame that comes with our sin. (Note: Even though shame has a short-term destructive effect on people, God uses it in the long run to draw people to Himself.)

Fathers take this condition, intensify it, and give it direction. Here's how many believe this dynamic works: God designed an incredibly strong bonding instinct as a survival mechanism that compels a child to attach to his primary caregivers (especially Dad). While locked in this relationship, the child discovers who he or she is by bouncing himself or herself off of the parents. The child picks up hints and clues about himself or herself by scrutinizing his or her own reflection as perceived in the eyes (the identity mirrors) of the parents.

The whole system backfires, however, if the parents themselves are shame-bound and are emotionally depleted from struggling with their own negative self-images. They are then unable to pour themselves into their children and can't meet the love needs required to develop a child's healthy self-concept. The child looks into the distorted mirrors of the parents that send back sick reflections, thus causing a flawed self-concept.

The child picks up on the rejection and concludes, "I am guilty." Guilt itself, however, is an objective historical fact of behavior. It tells me that I made a mistake. It is not me (identity); it is something I did (behavior). Guilt is the "legal and moral condition that results from a violation of God's law" (*Zondervan Encyclopedia*, Vol. II, Merrill C. Tenney, General Ed. [Grand Rapids: Zondervan, 1975], 852–53). Guilt tells me that what I did was wrong.

God designed guilt as a painful flashpoint to bring us to a quick insight and a rapid change of behavior. It's similar to sticking your finger into a flame: The pain instantly wises you up, causing you to jerk your hand away from the fire. Guilt should hurt. It should make you jerk away from what you are doing before you really damage yourself.

Guilt, however, can become a problem in itself. Instead of a friend to keep us out of trouble, guilt, left to fester, becomes an enemy. If we refuse to act quickly to its prompting, it can mutate into a chronic anguish called *shame*. Unresolved guilt can be converted into feelings of shame. Extended feelings of guilt make us believe we are a shameful person incapable of good behavior. Guilt multiplies our sense of shame and propels us around the shame-based cycle again.

At best, when the father showers the child with love and acceptance, the child feels better about himself or herself and grows up without too much damage. Not even the best father, however, can compensate or remove the effects of the sin/guilt/shame base passed down from Adam.

At worst, toxic fatherhood amplifies the poison of the inherited sin/guilt/shame base by constantly saturating the child with negative reinforcement and condemnation. Shame is added to shame at a deadly rate. This process causes the child to establish a destructive shame-based identity.

The problem comes when shame is intensified, reinforced, and internalized. When a child takes the feelings of guilt and shame and starts to build his or her identity out of them, the child has stepped over the line and has entered the destructive area of shame-basing. The child gets into trouble when he or she stops saying, "I *made* a mistake and *feel* a little ashamed!" and starts saying, "I *am* a mistake and I *am* a shame!"

This toxic shame is a fatal sickness of the soul. It is a soul wound—a tear, a rip in the soul fabric. Shame assassinates the soul and numbs the heart. It produces a psychic numbness that robs us of life and vitality.

Rejection, therefore, causes a child to feel chronic guilt, which develops into a shame-based heart. This rejection also leads to a large "pain pool" that overpowers the child.

Step Three: The "Pain Pool"

Shame hurts and causes great pain. When we experience shame, we see ourselves as undesirable and dishonorable. We feel ostracized, rejected, and abandoned. Since God designed us for love, the feelings of rejection are the most intensely painful feelings that humans can suffer. Suicide, therefore, is the highest note on the rejection scale.

This pain can easily overwhelm a child's ability to process it. This pain can also begin to collect in a child's heart to form a "pain pool." With time, the pool grows until it reaches flood stage and is ready to overflow with fury, causing personal damage and harm to others. (See Volume 1, *Dad the Family Coach* for more on the pain pool.)

Step Four: A Defensive Heart

When I know that I am defective and filled with shame, it hurts a lot, but there is one thing that hurts even more: for me to know that others know it too. I bleed when I face my shame, but I hemorrhage when others see it. When pain from shame and failed relationships builds to an intolerable level, a point is reached where one must kill the pain or go crazy. Shame-pain drives us to adopt certain behaviors that protect our hearts.

I call these behavioral disorders "blockers" (defense mechanisms) and "numb-ers" (pain killers). We use "blockers" to keep more pain from flowing into the pain pool. "Numb-ers" attempt to keep the pain in the pain pool from hurting so much. These disorders can take the form of mood-altering drugs and/or diversionary behaviors that form addictions, obsessions, and compulsions.

These compulsive/addictive behaviors numb the pain, but they work only for a short time. Then the dosage and frequency need to be increased. They also cause other problems that result in even more pain. Once you get into the cycle, you are trapped. One man has said, "I drink to solve the problems caused by being an alcoholic."

Incidentally, another word for all of these dysfunctional behavior patterns is sin. Sinful behaviors are those done apart from faith that result in damaged and fatal relationships with God, self, and/or others. You can't sin without damaging a relationship somewhere.

Blockers and numb-ers hide the heart, but they also put up barriers to healthy personal relationships.

Step Five: Distorted Relationships

As a child and for much of my early life, no one knew me or had any idea who I really was. For that matter, neither did I! With a personality centered on shame, transparency and intimacy became my enemies while secrecy and blockage became my soul mates. Psychological defense mechanisms covered me up and hid me. My behavior made it difficult for me to develop normal healthy relationships. People cannot love whom they do not know.

When a man hides behind blockers and numb-ers, the fear of discovery grows and the protection devices become more complex and difficult to maintain. Fear of discovery grows and causes movement toward further isolation. There is safety in aloneness. Movement toward isolation is a drift toward further unreality and different degrees of psychological and emotional problems. Healthy relationships become elusive while distorted relationships become the norm.

As he analyzes these distorted relationships, he reads failure, guilt, and shame. Meanwhile, more pain flows into the pain pool, and the cycle continues to become worse.

There must be a better way. There is! We can convert our shame-based identity to an honor-based identity.

MANAGEMENT BY HONOR

If you suspect that you or anyone in your family suffers from a sin/guilt/shame-based self-concept, you need to approach the problem with great wisdom. Be careful not to apply Band-Aids and cosmetics to symptoms because the problem is not guilt, codependent behavior, or distorted relationships. We must dig all the way down to the core of our being and make drastic changes in our personhood to clear up the other problems.

A shame-based person needs a heart transplant. Fortunately, this operation is possible through the work of Jesus Christ. In the Bible, the central point concerning humanity is that God developed a plan to transform sinful people with a shame-based heart into children of God with an honor-based heart.

This next section is the most important in the entire book because it tells you how to become the man you must be to be the father you want to be. Children do who you are, not what you say. Please get your Bible and study the passages listed below, reading my comments on how we can convert the sin/guilt/shame cycle into an honor/grace base.

Intended for Honor
Since God is love (1 John 4:16), He created us for fellowship with Himself. He intended for us to be His children and have fellowship with Him. Common sense and an honest look at history, however, tells us that, in spite of great accomplishments and traces of commendable traits, we neither share in God's nature nor act in ways that honor Him.

Humanity suffers from a moral defectiveness. We fall far short of God's holiness and righteousness, which we were intended to share with Him (Rom. 3:10-18, 23). In comparison to God, we are a blighted race, whom He has rejected (and rightfully so).

Something went wrong. According to the Bible, sin contaminates us all, having entered the human race through Adam and having been passed down to all of us (5:12-17). Every person is infected with sin, making us unfit for fellowship with God. We are not what we were originally intended to be. We became a sinful species. We are a fallen race. We neither have the meaning that should be ours nor do we accomplish our higher purpose as long as we remain who we are—ordinary humans (Eph. 2:1-3). We are unable to fellowship with God in our present state because we are so unlike Him.

The Barriers to Honor
To make things worse, we are trapped in our own little self-contained, four-dimensional world. We can't see the truth of the

extradimensional spiritual world (1 Cor. 2:14). This myopia restricts the scope of our search for value, meaning, and purpose in life. Deep inside, however, we instinctively know that there is more to life than what we do see and that we should be more than what we are (Rom. 1:20-21).

We also are instinctively aware of the spiritual kingdom, but we do not have the means to discover the reality of it. It is beyond our normal human perception. To put it into popular terms, we only have normal sensory perception with our five senses that pick up information from the physical world; we do not have extrasensory perception or paranormal psychic abilities with which to interpret data from the metaphysical realm. We don't have the capacity to see into the spiritual world.

We are like a baby in a womb. We exist fully alive but severely limited in a small dimensional world. Our knowledge of the outside world is severely restricted; yet, we instinctively know that it exists. Although we sometimes receive muffled signals that indicate the existence of a world outside the womb, we must wait until we are born into that world before we can experience it and discover a fuller meaning and purpose to life.

Since we are estranged from God, we do not grasp the reality and implications of being flawed creatures who are not as holy as God. Instead, we tend to compare ourselves to one another, measuring ourselves as better than the rest of humanity (Rom. 3:9).

People have always imagined that there is a supreme being who grades on a curve and accepts only exceptional humans who have passed a certain mark. Many other people in our culture believe God is more *humane*, taking those who sincerely try to do good. If there is a god, he is probably lenient and will receive all but the bottom 5 percent. These misconceptions make God far less than He is and humanity far more than it is. The difference between God and people is incredible, and only God can bridge the gap (Gal. 2:16).

Becoming a Christian is much more than adopting a self-improvement program or committing to a certain respectable lifestyle. Christianity is far more radical than most people realize. Even many Christians do not fully grasp the drastic measures required to convert a human into a person acceptable to God (Rom. 6:3-7).

Since sin has estranged us from God, He instills us with shame—a horrible, painful emotion that drives us through life looking for Him to find relief. Shame is a "locater" emotion: It hurts and keeps us moving until we get where we should be. We will struggle with shame until we cease being normal humans and change into children of God.

This is the central human dilemma: Sin controls us and separates us from God, and there is nothing we can do about it. We will die in our sin. Actually, we are already dead in our sin and dead to God since there is no life without Him (5:12; 6:23).

My Journey to Honor

Until my junior year at Georgia Tech, I was dead to God. Like a baby in the womb, I lived my life totally ignorant of the spiritual world outside this physical earth. I was cut off and blind to it. I did not have any apparatus that could extend into it and send back data. Since I didn't believe it existed, I concluded that there was no God.

I developed an atheistic mind-set: The world is time, space, matter, and energy, and nothing else. The only world is what I could personally observe and test—if I couldn't see it, it didn't exist. I ruled out the existence of the spiritual world because it could not be photographed, measured, chemically analyzed, or physically observed.

It seemed to me that God was a figment of human imagination and that people dreamed up God to explain mysteries they couldn't understand and to use Him as leverage to gain religious control over others. Intellectual, liberated, illuminated, and progressive people did not need myth-systems to help them shuffle through a dark and mysterious world. In fact, I thought religion had caused more damage and limited human progress more than anything else.

I did not see the absurdity of my position; for, in order to deny categorically the existence of God, I had to take an irrational leap by assuming that humanity possessed *all* knowledge and that I could demonstrate that God did not exist simply because I had not discovered Him. I denied the possibility that there was a sliver of datum tucked away in a secret corner of the universe that verifies God's existence.

At Georgia Tech, two men, John Battle and Jon Braun, challenged my closed system and presented me with credible verification for the existence of God and the spiritual world. They told me of their dynamic relationship with God and explained how I could meet God and develop a personal, eternal relationship with Him. (This experience is detailed in Volume 1, *Dad the Family Coach*, chapter 3.)

God's Plan for Honor

God, in His love and mercy, has taken the initiative and reached into our four-dimensional world with a message about eternal spiritual life. He provides a plan that allows us to know Him by getting rid of our sin and changing us into new beings with His nature and the capacity of fellowship with Him (Rom. 5:8-11). His solution calls for drastic measures: we are offered a choice of how to die. We can continue like we are, dead in our sins (Eph. 2:1), and live out our lives without a relationship with God. Or, we can put our faith in God's plan and die in Christ yet continue to live as a new creature in Him.

God's plan for us is shown on page 155.

1. Our sin keeps us spiritually dead.

Every person is born with sin and it keeps us dead to God and His truth. He is holy and righteous and will not allow any sin to come close to Him. He repels sin. If you have sin in you, you automatically get repelled with it—you can't get close to God. You exist as a human being, but you are dead spiritually. (See Rom. 3:23; 5:12; 6:23; Gal. 3:11.)

2. Christ endured spiritual death for us.

In His love and mercy, however, God has provided a plan that deals with our sin and changes us into new beings with the capacity to fellowship with Him. When Christ died on the cross, God took the sins of those who believe in Him and put them on Jesus. When Jesus took on our sins, He became a Sin-bearer like us. God therefore rejected His Son, who became a substitute sacrifice for us, dying in our place. Our sins caused a separation between Jesus and His Father. First Peter 2:24 says: "And He Himself bore our sins in His body on the cross, that we might die to sin and live to righteousness; for by His wounds you were healed." (Also see Rom. 4:25; 5:6, 8-11; 8:32; 1 Cor. 15:3; Heb. 9:26-28.)

3. With sin, the cause of spiritual death, removed, we can share spiritual life with God.

Here's how it works: If you believe in Christ, God places you in Christ while He was on the cross (handling your spirit and moving through time is no problem for God). You then die with Him, are buried with Him, and resurrected with Him.

Or do you not know that all of us who have been baptized into Christ Jesus have been baptized into His death? Therefore we have been bur-

154

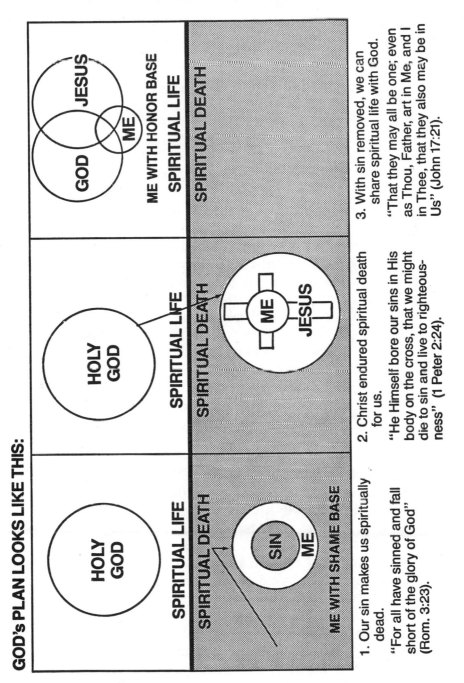

GOD's PLAN LOOKS LIKE THIS:

HOLY GOD — SPIRITUAL LIFE

SPIRITUAL DEATH — ME WITH SHAME BASE — SIN / ME

1. Our sin makes us spiritually dead.

"For all have sinned and fall short of the glory of God" (Rom. 3:23).

HOLY GOD — SPIRITUAL LIFE

SPIRITUAL DEATH — ME / JESUS

2. Christ endured spiritual death for us.

"He Himself bore our sins in His body on the cross, that we might die to sin and live to righteousness" (1 Peter 2:24).

GOD / JESUS / ME — ME WITH HONOR BASE — SPIRITUAL LIFE

SPIRITUAL DEATH

3. With sin removed, we can share spiritual life with God.

"That they may all be one; even as Thou, Father, art in Me, and I in Thee, that they also may be in Us" (John 17:21).

ied with Him through baptism into death, in order that as Christ was raised from the dead through the glory of the Father, so we too might walk in newness of life (Rom. 6:3-4).

This process converts us into a new species (2 Cor. 5:17). We are adopted out of the family of man into the family of God. This passage from being a normal human to a new being is so radical that it is like going from death to life and is compared to a birth. John even calls it the second birth (John 3:1-7). We are born into a new life and exist in oneness and unity in Jesus Christ, the Father, and the Holy Spirit (17:21-23).

This brilliant plan enables us to come alive to Christ and break the bondage that sin has over us (Rom. 6:14). We switch masters: Sin was our master, now Christ is (v. 16).

Thank God that He took the initiative and reached into my womb/world and told me the truth about the spiritual world. He converted spiritual truth and wisdom into terms that I can absorb and utilize. He used two mediums to reach me with the truth: the written Word (the Bible) and the Living Word (Jesus Christ). Man cannot extend himself into the spiritual world so God initiated direct contact with us to tell us things we could never find out for ourselves.

My conversion gave me a new identity core: I switched from a sinful shame-base to an honor-base in Christ. Since I am now sealed with the Holy Spirit (Eph. 1:13), merged into Christ (John 17:21-23) and a child of God (Rom. 8:16-17), I have a totally new identity. I no longer operate from a shame-base as a slave to sin. I am a new creature, the handiwork of God, and live with honor in Him.

Through the years, my growth in emotional and mental health has corresponded directly with the strength of my faith in my new identity in Christ. The more I realize who I am in Christ, the more I discharge all my horrible feelings of shame and discard my old habitual patterns of behavior and reactions. I have been in the process of exchanging my old set of damaging systems of coping for a new system of coping that produces life and peace.

Actually becoming a Christian is an instantaneous event that occurs when you trust Jesus as Savior by faith. The process of transforming your mind to line up with your new nature in Christ is a lifetime process that happens by faith. You put your faith in the power of the Holy Spirit and the Scriptures to work in you and bring you to maturity in Christ. Romans 12:2 says, "And do not be conformed to this world, but be transformed by the renewing of your mind, that you may prove what the will of God is, that which is good and acceptable and perfect."

There is no other way in the world for a person to undo the damage of a shame-base identity. Only a heart transplant can do it. For more insight into the process of changing a shame-base to an honor-base, read Robert McGee's book, *Search for Significance*.

ERASED BUT NOT ERADICATED

My awareness for the need of erasure which started as a child was the beginning of my struggle with the shame-based identity that eventually led me to a new life in Christ. I trusted Jesus as my Savior when I was a junior at Georgia Tech. Then I started the long process of healing and being refathered by my Heavenly Father.

Unfortunately, Dad reinforced the negative aspects of my shame to an extreme which caused me severe problems and more difficulty and pain in healing. But there is no man, woman, or child that is beyond the reach and healing touch of the Lord. He can reach into any person, no matter how damaged, and cause a rebirth into a new creature with eternal life in Him.

This chapter was included to help you realize the danger of building a shame-base into your children and how to help yourself and other family members get out of the trap and into the new life in Christ. You cannot be the father you want to be unless you become the son you were meant to be.

For more information on how to share these ideas with your children, see Volume 3, *Dad the Family Mentor*.

E-TEAM HUDDLE GUIDE
CHAPTER SEVEN:
Dad the Family Counselor

Dad, the Family Shepherd
E-TEAM

After coffee and fellowship, allow each dad to tell about the results of last week's project. This is the accountability part. Be firm with one another and encourage everyone to complete the project. If anyone encountered difficulty or had a family problem arise, pause to allow the E-Team to address the problem and pray.

E-TEAM DISCUSSION
50–60 minutes

This part allows you to discuss the key concepts in this chapter and relate them to your individual lives. Be sure to leave time to complete the workout and encouragement sections.

THE PRINCIPLES (Check the text for help.)
1. List and describe the steps in the Honor-Based Cycle and the Shame-Based Cycle.
2. What statement about current parenting does the epidemic in compulsive/addictive behaviors among young people make?
3. According to the Scriptures, what is God's plan to convert a shame-based person into an honor-based person?

THE IMPLICATIONS (Why are these ideas significant?)
4. Why are so many social and health programs designed to help compulsive/addictive people (alcoholics, drug addicts, sexaholics, and their codependents) doomed to fail? How do you know this?
5. Why is it essential for a man to become a son of God in order to maximize his potential as a father?
6. Explain the significance of the Cross in God's plan to adopt people into His family. What really happened on the cross and why did it have to happen? Be sure to base your answers on what the Scriptures say.

THE APPLICATION (How do these ideas affect me?)

7. What can I do to improve my ability to help my children achieve and strengthen an honor-base identity?

8. If you are a Christian, explain to the E-Team what benefits you have derived from Christ's work on the cross. Explain how you are a "new creature." Explain what it means to be one in Christ and share His nature and life with Him.

9. What do you have to be and what do you have to do to best help your children minimize their pain pool?

E-TEAM WORKOUT
10–15 minutes

Allow each dad to choose one of the project options (plays) to perform during the week. If desired, design your own project. Note: It is essential that each dad make a definite commitment to a specific project before he leaves.

1st PLAY:

If you are not a Christian, make this your project:

1. Read the Books of John and Romans a couple of times.
2. Make an appointment with your E-Team Captain or your pastor and ask them to go over the material at the end of this chapter with you.
3. Pray and ask God to tell you the truth about life and show you how you can become one of His sons.

2nd PLAY:

Make an appointment with your wife and discuss this chapter with her. Make a commitment to dedicate your family to Jesus Christ. Pray together. Start having a daily quiet time of fellowship with the Lord.

E-TEAM ENCOURAGEMENT
5–10 minutes

Close the meeting in prayer for one another and your families. Include in your prayer a specific request for spiritual power to complete your project successfully.

BREAK THE HUDDLE,
GO HOME AND RUN THE PLAY!

Chapter Eight
Dad the Family
Commander

"The true measure of a man is not what he
accomplishes, but what does it take to stop him."
— *Howard Hendricks*

FICKLE FINGERS OF FATE

One nice day, my dad whacked off the tips of three of his fingers with a lawn mower. He was stationed at Fort Bliss, and we were cutting the grass around the little home we lived in on the army post. After I had gone into the house for something, I heard a strange clicking sound and a howl from Dad. I rushed out back and saw him hopping around and holding his left wrist in a vise grip with his other hand. (Dad had the biggest hands I've ever seen: Shaking hands with him was similar to grabbing a bunch of bananas.)

Dark, heavy blood was spurting from his fingers, showering him and the back porch. I saw the gruesome sight of a severed fingertip, with a manicured fingernail, lying next to my foot. My father was in great pain, and through clenched teeth he barked out an order, "Dave, get in there and call the hospital and tell them what happened and that I'm on my way."

I instantly obeyed. His next order was for me to go into the bedroom and get his wallet and army I.D. card. He then said, "Now, get a pencil and paper and write a note to Mom and the girls and tell them I've had a serious accident, but that I'll be OK. Tell them to come to the hospital when they get home."

I scrambled around for a pencil and paper. I could hardly write. He was then out front and gave his final order, "Dave, get out in the street and flag me down a car." My mother had taken our only car.

The first two cars I stopped, the drivers saw all the blood and wouldn't let Dad in. The third car was an M.P. patrol car. He turned on his red light and siren and rushed us to the hospital. Meanwhile, Dad had made a tourniquet out of a belt and was trying to stem the flow of blood.

We reached the emergency room and Dad was wheeled immediately into surgery. The surgeons untangled his hamburger fingertips, discarded some parts, and molded the remaining pieces into patties, shaped like fingertips. They drilled bone, screwed pins, and stitched finger meat back together. He recovered but his left-hand fingertips were always a mess. You wouldn't want to hold hands with him.

I'll never forget the way my dad took command of the situation. I was always impressed with his ability to think clearly and make good decisions while he was in such pain. It had a lot to do with his training to make command decisions in a crisis as an army officer. I tried to copy this positive attribute. When I find myself in a crisis, I often think, "Now, how would Dad do this and what would he say?"

Dad had a great leadership profile. He knew how to carry himself with dignity and impressive military bearing. I was always impressed with Dad's ability to lead troops, handle his superior officers, make decisions, and accomplish missions. Dad was a powerful man, had received excellent training, and knew how to command troops.

The major flaw in Dad's family-management system was that he had only one command style. The military mode that made him successful as an officer followed him home, where he constantly stood his wife and children at attention. Dad did not know how to adapt his leadership expertise to family command. His command style was not flexible in handling the complexities of a wife, four children, and all the situations a family faces.

Wanted: Flexible Commanders

This chapter builds on Ephesians 6:4, which stresses the importance of effective command style:

> Fathers, don't use a command style that incites your children to rebellion and causes them to spin out of control, but be personally involved and use proper command style to nourish them up with God's principles of discipline and motivation (see Eph. 6:4).

Fathers are advised to use the right command technique or suffer rebellious results. This chapter deals with the different command styles of fathering. They might seem a bit complex and bulky for

161

family use at first, but I have found great success in not only using them with my family, but also in teaching them to my children while they were still in junior high school. And I have been using them ever since. Actually, these styles are based on commonsense ideas. By the way, they can be used in school, church, business, or anywhere there is a need for good leadership.

This chapter covers these topics:

The Command Complexity	How do you track the variables?
The Command Guide	How do you flex your style?
The Command Case Studies	How do you make it practical?

The Command Complexity

The difficulty in family command lies in the complex variables that swirl around the development of your "troops." If they were all the same age, same sex, at the same level of maturity, and if they shared common interests and understood command language like most G.I.s in a battalion, it would be a lot simpler.

Each child, however, constitutes a separate little world of unique variables that a commander must consider:

1. Age	5. "Bent" or nature
2. Sex	6. Sibling order
3. History or experience	7. Genetic endowment
4. Maturity	8. Situation

A good family commander takes all eight of these variables into consideration and modifies his command style to fit each unique situation exactly. The paternal perplexity is that the average dad must move a couple of children with eight variables each through ten developmental stages at different rates. Or, you can just club them continually with the same rigid style, no matter what.

A wise leader uses situational leadership; he does not use the same leadership style in every situation. A successful manager is one who has mastered the skill of matching each person/task situation with the appropriate command style. He makes two quick decisions before acting:

1. He evaluates the maturity of his followers in the context of the task.

2. He chooses one of four command styles to apply to the situation.

In this section we will discover how to evaluate followers in relation to the task and then how to choose the appropriate leadership style for that situation. We will use a management tool I call The Shepherd Command Chart, which I will explain. I then will provide some examples on how to use it in family situations.

I have borrowed the situational leadership quadrant concept from Blanchard and Hershey to explain situational leadership. I have adapted it as a management tool for family shepherds. (See *Management of Organizational Behavior*, Hershey/Blanchard, Prentice Hall, 1982, p. 152.)

The Family Shepherd Command Guide tells you what kind of leadership style to use with anyone in your family in any situation. The Family Shepherd Command Guide consists of three elements:

1. A Command Matrix that shows four leadership styles.
2. A Maturity Scale that relates people to the task.
3. A Command Curve that designates the appropriate leadership style for the situation.

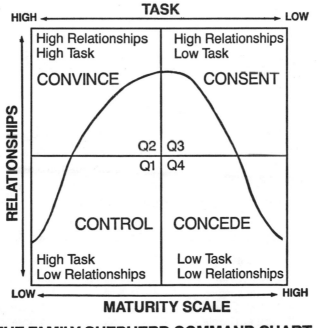

THE FAMILY SHEPHERD COMMAND CHART

THE COMMAND MATRIX

The Command Matrix is a matrix constructed by two variables: people (relationships are top priority) and task (the task is the top priority). The y axis measures people orientation that increases in an upward direction. The x axis measures task orientation that increases from right to left.

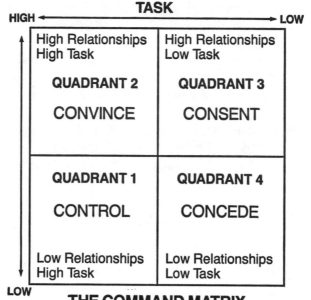

THE COMMAND MATRIX

Dividing the graph into quadrants makes for four leadership styles, each of which features a different ratio of people and task orientation. The people/task ratio of each quadrant describes a distinct command style. The Command Styles range from total exercise of authority to complete delegation of authority.

Table of People/Task Ratio to Command Style

Quadrant	People Orientation	Task Orientation	Command Style
Quadrant 1	Low People /	High Task	Control
Quadrant 2	High People /	High Task	Convince
Quadrant 3	High People /	Low Task	Consent
Quadrant 4	Low People /	Low Task	Concede

COMPARISON OF THE COMMAND STYLES

Q1 – Control Command
Description of Q1 – Control Command
1. Style: I tell them. Directive. Imperative.
2. Message: I show what and how.
3. Authority: I keep authority.
4. Responsibility: All mine.
5. Description: Q1 leadership puts a high premium on getting the job done and does not overly concern itself with the feelings and responses of the people. Q1 insists on achievement. It requires the job to be done, the quotas be filled, the standards be met and/or the parameters observed. The focus is on the leader and his goals.

Q1 leadership calls for a quick "control" command style. You must control the situation, no matter what, by any means required. There are no alternatives. You must make your command happen. You must be successful no matter what the cost. You carry complete responsibility and exercise total authority.

Orientation of Q1 – Control Command
1. Quadrant – Low people/high task.
2. Situations – Low Maturity in regard to task.

When followers do not have the knowledge, skill, desire, confidence, or commitment to carry out the task. They need to be walked through the whole process.

When followers face a life, death, and/or injury situation like a speeding truck bearing down on a child playing in the street, or a child about to step off of a high porch.

When crucial timing situations arise; like when you must get the family to the airport to catch a plane, you are trying to get a family portrait taken and you have already gone over your appointment time, or on Sunday morning and you are trying to get the family to the church on time.

Effects of Q1 – Control Command
1. Child's response: Obedience. "Control" commands in Q1 leadership require the family members to respond quickly with unquestioned obedience. Q1 does not allow for flexibility or individualism in the process.
2. Child's benefits – Learns self-control, submissiveness.

165

Coaching Tips for Q1 — Control Command
1. Reserve this for true emergency. The less used the better.
2. If possible, announce Q1 leadership before you commence to use it. You must alert the family to cue them for the appropriate response. For instance, you spot a tornado heading your way—just yell, "OK, kids, this is a 'Q1' command: Drop what you are doing and get into the house immediately."
3. Predetermine emergency situations and alert the children to coded Q1 commands. We have a standard Q1 command for an impending car wreck. If I ever shout, "Down!" the kids know we are about to wreck and throw themselves on the floor of the backseat automatically and Sandy, with her seat belt already on, thrusts her hands out toward the dashboard for extra protection.

Q2 — Convince Command

Description of Q2 — Convince Command
1. Style: I sell them. Influential, convincing.
2. Message: We discuss how and what.
3. Authority: We share authority.
4. Responsibility: We share responsibility.
5. Description: Q2 leadership puts a high premium on both the feelings and responses of your family members and on the achievement of the task you have in mind. Q2 leadership seeks to cultivate relationships and develop more interaction with the followers while still providing enough structure and supervision to insure task completion.

Q2 leadership requires you to "sell" the child on the idea and motivate him without seeming like a dictator. You dialogue with the child and get the child to adopt the task. You don't "make" the child; you motivate the child to make himself. You stick with the child until the task is done and your standards are met.

Orientation of Q2 — Convince Command
1. Quadrant: High People/High Task
2. Situations: Moderate Maturity in regard to task.

When your children are capable but are faced with tasks that are a little difficult or tedious. They need assistance in planning, getting started, and completing the task with excellence. Q2 tasks may include household chores, homework, music lessons, or church projects.

When your children are attempting new tasks and projects like constructing a doghouse, planning a vacation, or leading a church youth project.

Effects of Q2 — Convince Command
1. Child's response: Cooperation and commitment. "Convince" commands in Q2 leadership require the children to adopt the task as their own and feel like they accomplished it on their own and not because they were forced to. Q2 allows for flexibility and feedback from the children. They "work it out" with you and learn about teamwork, negotiation, and problem-solving. You are training them to think things out for themselves.
2. Child's benefits: Learns to think and plan.

Coaching Tips for Q2 — Convince Command
1. Always make your desired results specific and crystal clear.
2. In the dialogue to convince them of the need to accomplish the task, be sure to listen to their arguments sincerely and carefully. Keep your responses on their level and be as logical as possible. Lay out your logic on the table and make sure they follow it so they can learn to think logically. They may not agree but make sure they understand.
3. After all is said and done, be tactful when insuring that they buy into your decisions.

Q3 — Consent Command
Description of Q3 — Consent Command
1. Style: I participate. Sharing.
2. Message: I let you do it with my help.
3. Authority: I lend authority to you.
4. Responsibility: I share responsibility.
5. Description: Q3 leadership puts the emphasis on relationships and the task becomes a negotiable item. Q3 leadership insists on a serious merging process where the leader and the followers focus on team interaction even to the point where the team may redefine the tasks and standards. Unity becomes an unspoken goal: goals become flexible. Q3 describes real teamwork.

Q3 leadership calls for pooling your authority and responsibility with the other members of the team. Q3 leadership is participative leadership. You must be more flexible and permissive. Let the children do a lot of the thinking and concluding. Help them think through their solutions by asking questions and volunteering ideas. Bring them to a conclusion that is acceptable to you and give them permission to proceed. But stand close behind them so, if need be, they can consult you.

Orientation of Q3—Consent Command
1. Quadrant: High People/High Task.
2. Situations: Good Maturity in regard to task.

When children can adequately participate in a meaningful way in the planning process and a specific result is not essential. Examples: planning family projects, vacations or a weekend.

When a child is capable of doing a task without any help but wants to increase the efficiency or raise the standards.

Effects of Q3—Consent Command
1. Child's response: Teamwork.

"Consent" commands in Q3 situations require the children to join the team and interact with you and take more responsibility for planning the activities. As you give consent, they begin to take ownership and share the authority and the consequences with you.
2. Child's benefits: Learns leadership skills.

Coaching Tips for Q3—Consent Command
1. Look at Q3 as a team of peers working together to come up with a solution.
2. You can afford to be pretty democratic in Q3. Try to arrive at conclusions by consensus.
3. If you see they are headed for trouble, be as diplomatic as possible and participate by asking questions and try to get them to see the problems and make corrections. Avoid Q1 style at all costs. Nothing can cramp their development more than slashing across all of their best work and forcing them to do your bidding after all.

Q4—Concede Command
Description of Q4—Concede Command
1. Style: I delegate. Authorize, entrust.
2. Message: I let you do this without me.
3. Authority: I give authority away.
4. Responsibility: They take all responsibility.

Q4 leadership puts a high premium on turning the entire job over to the followers. It calls for you to delegate and turn loose. You have such confidence that you allow them to assume all authority. You inform them that they have full ownership and allow them to proceed with defining the task, setting goals, and developing procedures and standards.

Q4 leadership allows you the luxury of delegating the entire situation to the children. You let them take over and go for it. You communicate your complete trust and confidence in them to handle everything successfully. You must remain nondirective in task activities and assume little responsibility for interpersonal relations. You release authority and let them enjoy the consequences, whatever they may be.

Orientation of Q4 — Concede Command

1. Quadrant 4: Low People/Low Task.
2. Situations: Complete Maturity in regard to task.

When the children have passed driver's education and have established a proven track record, you allow them to drive to and from school and stop off at a friend's or the local teen hangout.

When children have demonstrated enough maturity for complete trust and competence where you can turn over activities like their household chores, school homework assignments, and money budgeting.

Effects of Q4 — Concede Leadership

1. Child's response: Take ownership.

"Concede" commands in Q4 situations allow you to concede all authority and responsibility to the children and turn loose completely.

2. Child's Benefits: Learns to take initiative.

Coaching Tips for Q4 — Concede Command

1. Make sure the children understand the limits of the authority you concede to them. For instance, you may wish to limit the car mileage per week, or allow them a measured amount of time to do chores or put some purchasing restrictions into effect.
2. Try never to go back on your word and take back authority. Authority granted becomes authority almost impossible to reclaim. If you ever anticipate having to step back in, define the intrusion

criteria from the outset so they know you are playing by the rules.

THE MATURITY SCALE

You must first determine the performance maturity of your child in relation to the task in order to locate the correct Command Quadrant. This determination requires consideration of numerous data about the child in relation to that task. After you process the data, it should take you to a fairly close estimation of his or her maturity level; but when you get right down to it, you must rely on your own judgment.

Among the things to consider in estimating the maturity level of your child, you need to think through the following five areas:

1. The child's design

Is the child suited for the task by nature? Does the child have a "bent" that fits the requirements of the task? Does the task require a certain temperament or personality type that fits your child? Does your child have the spiritual gifts required?

2. The child's ability

Does the child have the necessary knowledge to accomplish the task? Can he or she understand the commands and instructions? Can the child follow the instructions?

Does the child have the necessary skill to tackle the task? Does he or she have adequate dexterity, coordination, and motor skills? Is he or she physically strong enough? Conditioned enough?

3. The child's desire

Does the child have the necessary confidence to approach this task? The child doesn't have to be totally confident—you don't have to shield him or her from challenges and fear. Is the task, however, so awesome to the child that it will intimidate him or her and insure failure?

Does the child have the necessary commitment? Does he or she understand why the task must be done? Does the child understand the consequences of success and failure? Does the child feel as though his or her motivational needs will be met if the task gets done?

4. The child's durability

Does the child have the necessary resources to survive and/or persevere in case the task fails? How serious are the consequences of failure? Death? Injury? Loss of family? Can the child respond to the urgency or importance of the situation?

5. The child's position

Does the child possess the appropriate status and relationship to others to fill his or her assigned role for the task? Does the task fall within the gender-role parameters and/or age-role limits of the child?

After you have determined the maturity level of your child in regard to the task, you indicate your result on the Shepherd Command Chart by putting a dot on the Maturity Line at the top of the chart. The level of maturity increases from low to high as it moves from left to right.

0%	25%	50%	75%	100%

- -

low maturity   **high maturity**

Here are some examples of how to determine the maturity level in regard to the task:

1. Helen was fifteen and chomping at the bit to drive. Since she had never driven before, I rated her extremely immature and located her at the left edge of the maturity line at about 5 percent. When she was eighteen, I rated her around 80 percent. After she had a few bumps and wrecks, I dropped her down to 60 percent. Now she's way up again.

2. Although Helen was only fifteen, because she had gone through our camp "Training N Teamwork" course so often and done so well, I rated her extremely mature and located her on the right edge of the line near the 97 percent point.

3. When Helen was twenty, she showed incredible leadership and organizational skills, but she had a hard time with details and administration. In evaluating her to be the girl's camp director, I located her at about 75 percent mature for the task.

4. When Helen started cleaning the bathroom, she had great ability, but her heart wasn't in it. Thus, I located her at about 35 percent.

5. When Brandon started going out as a teenager, I rated him very low. Since he never missed curfew, however, I raised him to 50 percent. He continued to do very well, and I soon rated him in the 90 percent area.

6. When Helen first started riding horses at around three years old, she was definitely a 5 percenter. As she matured, so did her rating.

She had to pass the 98 percent mark before I made her head wrangler at the Ranch.

THE COMMAND CURVE

How does a family shepherd actually find out which command style to use in any given situation? How do you decide when to "control," "convince," "consent," or "concede"? The command curve tells you. To use the command curve to determine the appropriate command style, follow these steps:

1. Evaluate the maturity level of the child.
2. Locate the maturity level with a dot on the maturity line.
3. Trace a line from the maturity-level dot straight down until it intercepts the bell-shaped command curve.
4. The point where the line hits the command curve places you in a certain quadrant. The quadrant tells you which command style to use.

COMMAND STYLE CASE STUDIES

Case Study 1: Helen's Driving Adventures.

Her first rating was at 5 percent (A). Locate 5 percent on the maturity scale and drop a line straight down. It hits the command curve in Q1. Therefore, I used Q1 — Control Command. This means that I am in complete control. I ride shotgun and tell her everything to

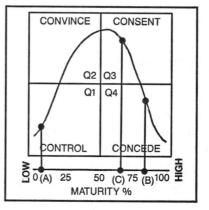

do with short snappy commands, and I expect instant obedience.

When she was rated at 80 percent (B), the line hit the command curve in the Q4. Therefore, I used Concede Command. I let her take the car out anywhere at anytime. I entrusted her with complete authority and permitted her to take complete ownership.

After she totaled Sandy's ten-year-old Datsun, we brought her back down to 60 percent (C) which is in Q3 — Consent Command. She had to have one of us ride with her and share responsibility. She soon proved herself again and now has her own car.

Case Study 2:
Helen's T.N.T. Privileges.

The T.N.T. course is an advanced teamwork course that my friend, Roc Bottomly, installed at King's Arrow Ranch to equip our college counselors. Helen excelled as she competed in it as a junior high student. By the time she was fifteen, she knew the principles and team dilemmas

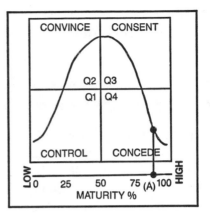

cold. She has the gifts of discernment, insight, and counseling; so when she asked to be a Team Observer and critique the college students, I rated her in the high 90s (A). I dropped down my line from the maturity scale and ended up in Q4—Concede Command. I gave her a T.N.T. clipboard and evaluation sheets and turned her loose. She did great, and the college students accepted and responded to her.

Case Study 3:
Helen, the Girl's Camp Director.

Helen possesses great "public" gifts. She demonstrates excellent public speaking and crowd-control abilities. She has superior intuition and a "feel" for working with groups of kids. She thinks well on her feet, can solve problems, and handle emergencies extremely

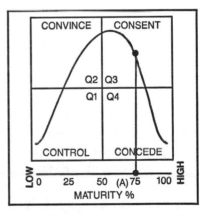

well. She is, however, just like me when it comes to administrative details. She hates records, checkbook stubs, desks, and all paperwork.

When it came time to consider her for Girl's Camp Director, therefore, I rated her high in most areas, but I shot her down in the administrative and record-keeping departments. Since I placed her maturity level at 75 percent (A) in Q3 command, I kept an eye on her. I let her do it, but I made sure she had good help in her weak areas.

Case Study 4:
Sandy Trains Them Young.

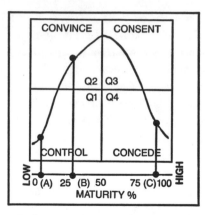

Sandy had Helen in charge of cleaning the bathroom when she was five years old. Her first few times, she simply watched Sandy demonstrate. Then Sandy stood by her and watched her through every step, guiding and correcting her. Since she rated a 5 per-

cent (A) at the time, Sandy used Control Command. As Helen improved, so did her rating, and Sandy started backing away. Cleaning toilets never captured Helen's imagination and ranked last on her list of fun things to do, right after changing diapers, which barely beat out suicide. So, even though she had the skills to rate in the 90s, she usually performed around 35 percent (B) and required close supervision. As she got older, she learned to work better and now pegs down about a 95 percent (C) in dirty household work.

Case Study 5:
Brandon's Curfew.

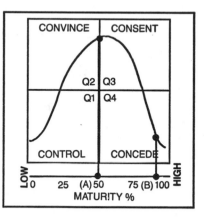

From the time Brandon first started "goin' out," he earned a reputation for always being home on time. He never missed curfew. I rated him at 50 percent (A) and gave him the freedom of staying out past curfew if he would call us and tell us what was happening. Soon, I gave him a high-90 rating (B)

because he always demonstrated good judgment and dependability. I turned his curfew over to him during his senior year in high school. I delegated authority to him and let him assume full responsibility for his daily schedule and curfew. He didn't have to call, and he could come in when he chose. He always used good sense and never got into any trouble.

If he had started drinking, or bothering other parents, or getting into fights, or hot-roddin' it, I would have yanked him back down to Q1 and made him double-date with Sandy and me!

Case Study 6: Helen and Her Horses.

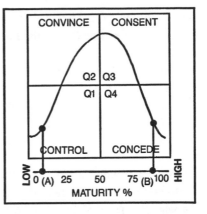

The first time I ever put her on a horse, she flipped off backward and buried her upper teeth in the dirt. She then was three years old. I had put her on her Shetland pony, Little Bit, and held her as the pony walked around the ranch house. It didn't take long for me to push her limits and let go of her. After Little Bit bolted for the barn, Helen belted the ground. Her nose and gums were bleeding, and I spent an hour picking sand granules out of her gums with a toothpick.

She rated about a 5 percent (A) then. (So did I! I should have had someone supervising me with strong Q1.) Eventually, Helen became the head wrangler, taught horsemanship to all the campers, and took them on long trail rides all by herself. She even took out overnight horse rides. She now rates a 98 percent (B) as an expert, and she has her own mare and colt.

THE DELTA 88 COMMANDER

Considering the time I barreled backward around Ft. Bliss in El Paso in the Oldsmobile, you may ask, "How should Major Amos have commanded his sixteen-year-old boy and the Delta 88?" Easy. Piece of cake. He should have given me the keys and asked me to borrow it when he needed it!

Seriously, when I asked for the keys, we were both in a no-win situation. Dad should have let me have the car because a boy needs to take his girl out once in a while. But, Dad should *not* have let me have the car because I was deceitful, untrustworthy, undependable, and irresponsible. We were stuck in a quagmire that had been hardening for sixteen years and that had finally trapped us both.

The good Ole Major should have prepared his son to drive the

Olds about ten years before the boy first asked for the keys. You can't deal with teenagers when they are teenagers. The best time to deal with teens is when they are under ten years old.

If Dad had spent sixteen years working me around the Command Curve, through Q1-Q2-Q3-Q4, in a variety of areas of my life, we would have developed an understanding and trust that are so essential in the teen years. I could have gradually worked my way up to handle more responsibility. I could have enjoyed the privilege of earning my own progress. I could have had confidence that Dad wouldn't let me tackle something I couldn't handle.

Dad could have rested, confident that he had trained me to handle the authority and responsibility he had given me and that I wouldn't abuse his trust. He could have raised a son whose heart wasn't a seething cauldron of bitterness, rebellion, and hate.

Instead, we both became the opposite of what we wanted. I had no wheels, and Dad had no peace. We both lost.

E-TEAM HUDDLE GUIDE
CHAPTER EIGHT:
Dad the Family Commander

E-TEAM REVIEW
10–15 minutes

After coffee and fellowship, allow each dad to tell about the results of last week's project. This is the accountability part. Be firm with one another and encourage everyone to complete his project. If anyone encountered difficulty or had a family problem arise, pause to allow the E-Team to address the problem and pray.

E-TEAM DISCUSSION
50–60 minutes

This part allows you to discuss the key concepts in this chapter and relate them to your individual lives. Be sure to leave time to complete the workout and encouragement sections.

THE PRINCIPLES (Check the text for help.)
1. Explain how the Family Shepherd Command Guide works and how to use it to find out what kind of leadership style to use in a given situation.
2. Describe the following leadership styles:
    Control
    Convince
    Consent
    Concede

THE IMPLICATIONS (Why are these ideas significant?)
3. Why is it important to master a flexible leadership style? Why is it dangerous to be stuck in one leadership style?

THE APPLICATION (How do these ideas affect me?)
4. Discuss your father's leadership style and how it affected you.
5. Discuss your leadership style and how you can improve it.
6. How does your leadership style affect your wife? Your children?
7. How do you feel about the progress you are making in improving

your fatherhood skills since you joined the E-Team? Tell the E-Team about any positive feedback you have received from your family. What is the most important thing you have learned in the E-Team? 8. Discuss the possibility of taking the next course, *Dad the Family Mentor*, together as an E-Team. (It is entirely dedicated to child teaching and discipline.)

E-TEAM WORKOUT
10–15 minutes

Allow each dad to choose one of the project options (plays) to perform during the week. If desired, design your own project. Note: It is essential that each dad make a definite commitment to a specific project before he leaves.

1st PLAY:
Evaluate your ability to flex your leadership style. Choose one situation with each child and use the Family Shepherd Command Guide.

2nd PLAY:
Make an appointment with your wife. Discuss the flexible leadership principles. Show her the Family Shepherd Command Guide. Brainstorm on ways you can use it with your children.

3rd PLAY:
Pray about taking the next course, *Dad the Family Mentor*, with your E-Team. It covers how to teach, train, track, and tend your children. Or, you may want to become an E-Team Captain and lead your own E-Team through *Dad the Family Coach*.

E-TEAM ENCOURAGEMENT
5–10 minutes

Close the meeting in prayer for one another and your families. Include in your prayer a specific request for spiritual power to complete your project successfully. Also, pray about starting the E-Team up again to complete the third course in this series, *Dad the Family Mentor*.

BREAK THE HUDDLE,
GO HOME AND RUN THE PLAY!

The Extra Point

Dear Fathers,

This final point I leave you with: The world needs more long-distance dads—we have enough 100-yard-dash dads. Now that you have seriously begun your fathering enhancement process, go for the long-range system, not the quick fix. Finish what you have begun.

You have just finished Fatherhood 102, *Dad the Family Counselor,* the second course in the Dad the Family Shepherd Fatherhood Institute. This course covers three of the Four Fatherhood Functions: "To Love," "To Bond," and "To Lead."

The next course, Fatherhood 103—*Dad the Family Mentor,* covers, in great detail, the last of the Four Fatherhood Functions—"To Equip." This topic deals with the common functions associated with "child-raising" and "child discipline." This Fatherhood Function is a process that includes four steps, and each step has two chapters. The steps are:

$$\text{To Teach} \qquad \text{To Train} \qquad \text{To Track} \qquad \text{To Tend}$$

The next course gets into the nitty-gritty details of "How to equip your children" to get the most out of life. Actual coaching tips and refined techniques on this function are spelled out in a style that helps you easily grasp and use them in your fathering style. The next course takes you out on the practice field and lets you knock a little.

The Personal Fathering Profile continues to receive specific treatment in the next course. The dimension of Involvement is discussed and the three Strong Father Factors that go with it are explained fully.

Take encouragement that we will not be denied: Those of us who want to master fatherhood will have the heart and master the skills to do so. We have the assurance of Malachi 4:5-6:

> Behold, I am going to send you Elijah the prophet before the coming of the great and terrible day of the Lord. And he will restore the hearts of the fathers to their children, and the hearts of the children to their fathers, lest I come and smite the land with a curse.

So, go for it. Continue your E-Team and perfect your fathering style.

Sincerely,

Dave Simmons

Appendix A

Dad, the Family Shepherd

E·TEAM

Review of Volume One
Dad the Family Coach

This book, *Dad the Family Counselor*, is the second of three volumes in the *Dad the Family Shepherd* series and should be read only after first reading Volume 1, *Dad the Family Coach*. Much of the meaning, even the selection of topics, of this volume will make sense only after reading the first volume.

To help put this volume in context, I have included this short review of the main ideas in Volume 1, *Dad the Family Coach*.

SERIOUS FATHERHOOD
(Volume One—Chapter 1)

Fatherhood has awesome significance outside our own personal experience and interests. Fatherhood is a central theme of the Bible. God tells us that the performance of fatherhood plays a major role in His plan for the ages and for the health and safety of individual nations.

Fatherhood is the means God intends the truth about Himself to be passed down through the generations. He has given fathers the assignment and the unique, mysterious ability (father power) to carry out this plan. God gave men father power in order to transfer the Gospel down through at least four generations of their descendants.

The Fourth Generation Rule does not distinguish between good and evil. The energy of father power picks up the heart of a man, good or evil, and hurtles it down through his seed. Father power, therefore, can act as a negative force or a positive force. A father can send the light of God down through the next four generations, or he can send the darkness of sin down through the next four generations.

Dad the Family Counselor, you must understand father power and the Fourth Generation Rule and the dynamics of how your fathering style stimulates children the way it does and use it to advantage with your family.

COORDINATED FATHERHOOD
(Volume One—Chapter 2)

Each family is a living organism, a unique entity, a personal life-form with a distinct personality and character derived from its two major components—the roles (the people) and the rules (the systems). Each family exists as a unique entity with its own identity, character, social system, structure, secrets, rules, ethics, and habits. Each one has its own way of facing adversity, coping with stress, resolving conflict, solving problems, and defending itself. Each one has its own habits of hygiene, recreation, and revitalization. They all age and die in their own way. Together, these elements give the family its own peculiar personality.

The family gets its personality from the members and the members get their personality from the family. The family is both cause and causal: the members contribute to the formation of the whole and the whole clearly marks the individual. Yet each individual is unique and self-contained with personal identity and boundaries.

Any force that touches one part causes an energy transfer to all other parts and change results throughout the whole structure. There is no independent action and no isolated unaffected parts. The whole works its will on each part and each part determines the whole.

Healthy families allow each person to develop uniquely and reach full interdependent maturity. Dysfunctional families blur the distinction between members and clump together in unhealthy codependency. They all stay caught up in each other's dysfunctions.

SPIRITUAL FATHERHOOD
(Volume One—Chapter 3)

There are two sides to fatherhood: Who you *are* and what you *do*. Your character and personhood matters more than your fathercraft and daddy techniques. A family shepherd is careful to BE the right man as well as DO the right things.

The Bible points out this double responsibility clearly in Psalm 78:72— "So he shepherded them according to the integrity of his heart, and guided them with his skillful hands."

Competent shepherding entails two essential aspects: your heart and your skills. You must have a heart of integrity, that is, you must BE a certain kind of man. You must DO specific activities that require a skillful hand.

It's not enough to just tackle the skills and techniques and bypass the development of your character. A man can be dysfunctional and master the Four Fatherhood Functions, then wonder why his family comes crashing down around him.

I give you now a major point of my concept of fatherhood: Children do what you are, not what you say. Who you are, the kind of man you are, is more important than all of your tasks, techniques, and talks. Children play with your words but work off your heart. Out of your heart come the issues of life and that's the true source of wisdom to a child.

You need to make sure your heart is right with God. You must know God personally through Jesus Christ and allow His Spirit, the Holy Spirit, to change your heart and empower you to reach your full potential for fatherhood. The best father you can be is the best son you can be. You must be a son of God to be the best father for your child.

RESPONSIBLE FATHERHOOD
(Volume One—Chapters 5–8)

Many fathers are demoralized because they can't get a grip on the overall scope of fatherhood and what their responsibilities are. No father can feel secure unless he knows exactly what he is supposed to do, how to do it, and how well it must be done. Therefore, I have gleaned the Scriptures and condensed all the tasks of fatherhood into four major groups and formatted them into a Fatherhood Job Description that has two major components—fatherhood style and fatherhood functions.

The Fatherhood Style

The Bible predicts that certain styles of fatherhood automatically produce confusion and rebellion. This passage explains what happened between Dad and me. "And, fathers, do not provoke your children to anger; but bring them up in the discipline and instruction of the Lord" (Eph. 6:1-4).

I have paraphrased this passage to read like this:

> Fathers, don't use a command style that frustrates your children and incites them to automatically rebel against you and your value system and spin out of control. Instead, use God's wisdom, be personally involved and use proper command style to nourish them up with biblical principles of discipline and motivation.

The Fatherhood Job Description

The Dad the Family Shepherd job description presents the four fatherhood functions. These functions and the roles are listed below.

Chapter	Function	Role
Five	To Love	Dad the Family Priest
Six	To Bond	Dad the Family Coach
Seven	To Lead	Dad the Family Man
Eight	To Equip	Dad the Family Mentor

Volume 1, *Dad the Family Coach* gives introductory material on each of these functions. This volume, *Dad the Family Counselor*, expands the first three and gives detailed coaching tips and techniques.

Appendix B

A Brief Synopsis of the Three Fatherhood Functions Covered in This Volume

THE FATHERHOOD FUNCTION: TO LOVE

SYNOPSIS OF "TO LOVE"	
Function	To Love
Role	Dad, the Family PRIEST
Benefit	SIGNIFICANCE
Penalty	MEANINGLESSNESS
"To Love" answers the child's question: "What am I worth?"	

> Love is a mind-set that chooses to give the gift of self for the benefit of others regardless of their performance.

There are two kinds of love: natural love and spiritual love. All humans are born with Natural Love but a person is able to get Spiritual Love when he trusts Jesus Christ as Savior. When Jesus enters a life, He takes His type of love with Him.

Love is action, sacrificial action. Love is a concrete transaction that converts your attitude into the currency of beneficial discernable action that benefits another person.

You are to love your family with the same kind of love with which Christ loved the church. He acted out His love as a living sacrifice—nourishing, cherishing, and eventually dying for the sake of the church.

THE ROLE: DAD THE FAMILY PRIEST

God created children as love seekers with a built in urgent need for love and assigned you the function of meeting this need. You plant love, cultivate it, nourish it and harvest it in your family. Love is the dominant characteristic of a priest. Jesus, the High Priest, so loved the church that He gave Himself up for her. In a similar manner, Dad the Family Shepherd functions as a loving priest.

THE BENEFIT: SIGNIFICANCE

Love establishes significance. When you love, the other person increases in value and worth. Love transfers your significance to the other person. Example: Jesus loves you and died for you which makes you extremely valuable and significant.

You, as family shepherd, humble yourself and love your children, you assign significance to your children. Your unconditional love acknowledges the importance and worth of family members. It allows them to develop a stable, positive self-esteem and builds their confidence. Love and acceptance helps remove fear of rejection. Nothing makes them feel more significant and valuable than your love.

THE PENALTY: MEANINGLESSNESS

Without the perception of fatherly love, a child will experience feelings of meaninglessness. A neglected child will think, "I am unworthy and lack value. If I were significant, Dad would pay attention to me. I must be defective, blemished, faulty. He ignores me or only notices me when I do wrong or bad. I will never measure up and be worthy of Dad's care."

THE FATHERHOOD FUNCTION: TO BOND

SYNOPSIS OF "TO BOND"	
Function	To BOND
Role	Dad, the Family COACH
Benefit	BELONGINGNESS
Penalty	ALONENESS
"To Bond" answers the child's question: "Where do I belong?"	

Bonding is the creative art of deep knowing and skillful placing of each person into a special niche to form a whole where everyone's needs for belongingness are met.

Bonding allows the father to help his family know that they belong and fit in a special place in the family. You are like a coach who helps his players know where they belong and work together like a team. You, as Dad the Family Shepherd, are responsible for the depth and quality of bonding in your family. It starts with the quality of your relationships with your wife and carries over to parent/child bonding.

Bonding is the creative art of deep knowing and skillful placing of each person into a special niche to form a whole. You are responsible for bonding your family together in a perfect pattern of togetherness. You preside over the unification of the family and make sure each member fits into the whole and feels belongingness. You keep them going and make them feel like part of the team.

THE ROLE: DAD THE FAMILY COACH

Your family needs a coach. You, the family coach, must be there and focus intently on building your family into a team where they all rest securely in feelings of belongingness.

The magic word in coaching is teamwork. Teamwork wins games. Winning coaches know how to take a group of individual players, put them in exactly the right position and motivate each to make his maximum contribution. The coach must have keen insight into each player, a thorough knowledge of what each position requires, and then he matches the players to the position. When you know each member intimately, you can help them settle into their position, learn the basics, and start making their maximum contribution to the team.

THE BENEFIT: BELONGINGNESS

Belongingness is the deep need all of us have for affiliation and attachment. God created us as sentient beings of attachment. The human soul was never intended to exist alone feeling aloneness. God wants us to bond with Him and He created the family as a training exercise with which to perfect the skills of bonding. Family members bond with each other to avoid the profound despair that comes with isolation.

THE PENALTY: ALONENESS

The ultimate core of the soul of man cries out to belong. God made us that way. We were not intended to suffer the separation of soul from our body (earthly death), or the soul from God (spiritual death) or our soul from others (social death). All of our attempts at relationships are efforts to make contact with others and alleviate the pain of separation. Our ability to bond determines our level of success at relationships. Without a family that bonds and a father who sets the pace for bonding, a child grows up without the experience and model to copy.

Such a child will suffer the effects of isolation more than ever. He will never feel like he belongs. He will always feel like he is on the outside looking in. No matter how many clubs, teams, organizations, groups, or societies his name appears on, he will not feel like he belongs. Not only will he not feel like he belongs, he won't know that something is missing. He knows that others are different, but he won't know how.

Lack of bonding tears the soul and causes major destructive behaviors. In poorly bonded homes, children are much more prone to get involved in illegal drugs and premarital intercourse. The risk increases even more when the father moves out of the family.

Lack of bonding causes pain and trouble. Of all the tortures ever divised, many break the body but the one that eventually breaks the mind is isolation. Prisoners, castaways, sentinels and astronauts complain most of the haunting fear that comes from the choking aloneness.

THE FATHERHOOD FUNCTION: TO LEAD

SYNOPSIS OF "TO LEAD"	
Function	To LEAD
Role	Dad, the Family MAN
Benefit	IDENTITY
Penalty	ANONYMITY
"To Lead" answers the child's question: "Who am I?"	

A leader is one under authority who provides stability, knows what to do next, and can motivate his team to work together to accomplish a task with maximum efficiency while building unity.

You are assigned the prime authority in your home. You are God's steering wheel for the family, His control instrument. You are the "face" of the family who sees the vision and purpose of the family. You hold the position in the family that insures that the family stays on track and functions as God's smallest battle formation.

THE ROLE: DAD THE FAMILY MAN

Be a man: be a father. Let your wife represent femininity. A man should be a male and a woman makes a better female and never the twain shall meet. A child doesn't need a set of androgynous interchangeable bookend parents. A child must be exposed to a masculine father and a feminine mother in order to establish a healthy rewarding gender-identity.

Of course, many functions of fathers and mothers are interchangeable but a definite maleishness and femaleishness needs emphasis. Who and how you are as a male counts as much as doing the deeds. You are a father, not just a parent.

THE BENEFIT: IDENTITY

As Dad, the family head, you function as the presenting figurehead of the family. You are its major source of identification. It goes by your name. Since you are the family "representative," "control knob" and "face," you provide a symbol or logo of the family. As such, each family member defines personal identity in relation to you. You help each member establish personal identity.

Whereas you tend to identify yourself with your job, your wife tends to identify herself with you. Your children are born with no self-concept and begin taking all their cues on self-identity from you. They voraciously read you and interpret you into a new unique expression. Even when they soak up identity from Mom, they still absorb you because so much of your wife's identity is constructed from you.

THE PENALTY: ANONYMITY

Children without a strong father in the home grow up with poor ego-strength. The term anonymity, the state of being unknown or obscure, describes how they feel. They feel like they are irrelevant superfluous, and expendable. They don't matter. Paternally deprived children feel defective, incompetent, inept, and useless.

These feelings are extremely painful because they run cross grain to how our human psyche was constructed. God did not create us to exist as unknown or obscure creatures. He knows each one of us down to the hairs on our heads. We are not nameless microscopic motes of dust. God created us in His image and we were meant to reflect His stature and dignity.

Appendix C

Dad the Family Shepherd Resources

THE E-TEAM CAPTAIN'S GUIDE

This E-TEAM **Captain's Guide** provides you with everything you need to lead an E-Team study of this book. This manual is in the appendix of Volume One: *Dad the Family Coach* or you can order it from Dad the Family Shepherd.

THE VIDEO CONFERENCE

The three volumes in the Dad the Family Shepherd Series originated out of the live conference that Dave Simmons has been teaching since 1984. The conference, entitled *Build Your House on the Rock*, covers not only fatherhood but other critical issues that men must face.

This conference is now available on video. The video package is designed to be used for conferences and is not for sale. You or your church must schedule a conference and use the video for the presentation. Schedule one anytime, anyplace, for any number. There is no minimum attendance required as in the live conference.

THE FATHERHOOD INSTITUTE

The Fatherhood Institute is a comprehensive fatherhood training process. It is designed and packaged so a church can easily adopt it and adapt it to their unique situation and equip their men to become more effective family shepherds.

It features a curriculum of eight-week courses and is formatted for small groups of men called Encouragement Teams (E-Teams). Fathers make a commitment for one course at a time and the courses are offered on a trimester basis — fall, winter, and spring.

FATHERHOOD RESOURCES

We at Dad the Family Shepherd have consolidated a collection of books, tapes, assessment instruments, and other helpful tools to help you excel in fatherhood. For a catalog of our resources and for more information on the Video Conference and the Fatherhood Institute, contact:

Dad the Family Shepherd
P.O. Box 21445
Little Rock, AR 72221
(501) 221-1102